TRANSFORMING COMPLEX TRAUMA

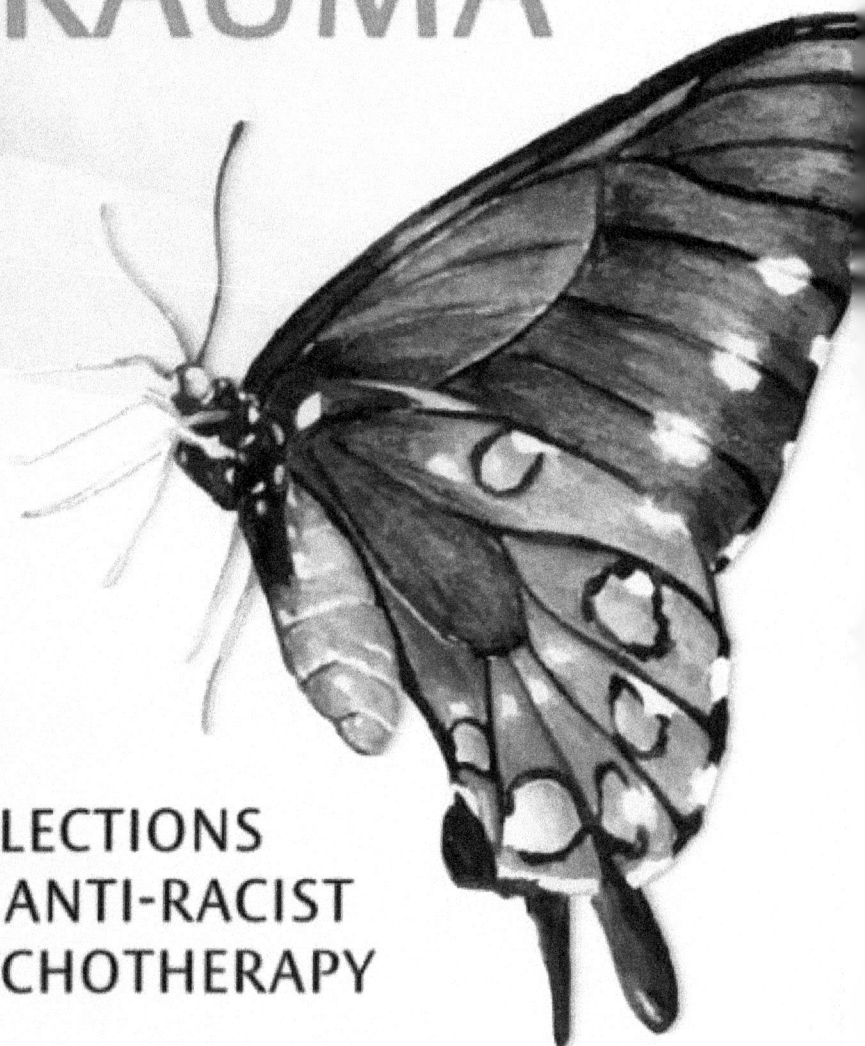

REFLECTIONS ON ANTI-RACIST PSYCHOTHERAPY

DAVID ARCHER

TRANSFORMING
COMPLEX TRAUMA
REFLECTIONS ON ANTI-RACIST PSYCHOTHERAPY

DUPPY
KONKARA
PUBLICATIONS

DAVID ARCHER, MSW, MFT

TRANSFORMING COMPLEX TRAUMA: REFLECTIONS ON ANTI-RACIST PSYCHOTHERAPY

Note: All individuals presented in story segments are based on composites. Fictional descriptions have been used in order to maintain confidentiality. The information provided in this book should not be treated as a substitute for professional medical or clinical advice. Always consult a medical professional and/or clinical practitioner. Any use of this book is at the reader's discretion and risk. Neither the author nor the publisher can be held responsible for any loss, claim, or damage arising out of the use, or misuse, of the content in this book, or from the failure of the reader to seek or take medical and/or clinical advice upon reading this book. Similarly, neither the author nor the publisher can be held responsible for any loss, claim, or damage arising out of the use or misuse of any content accessed from third-party websites or references made as part of the content in this book, or from the failure of the reader to seek or take medical and/or clinical advice upon reading said third party content.

Disclaimer: By writing this book, neither the author nor publisher is engaged in providing psychological, medical, or any other form of treatment or advice. The ideas expressed in this book are not proposed to be a diagnosis of any condition, nor a cure for any mental health, psychological, or emotional condition or concern. All individuals who require a consultation, amelioration, and/or treatment for their mental health, other medical, or other well-being concerns should seek an individualized and thorough assessment by a licensed and registered physician or mental health professional and follow the advice received from such professionals without relying on the contents of this book for decisions and actions taken with regard to their personal health and well-being. For greater certainty, the author and publisher are not responsible for any negligence or wrong-doing committed by mental and other health care practitioners who read this book. These professionals are responsible for ensuring their practice with patients and clients follows all rules of professional conduct, competency standards, regulatory and other legal requirements applicable to the exercise of their professional judgement, skill, and expertise in their field of treatment and therapy.

First Printing: December 2023
Second Printing: February 2024
Third Printing: June 2024
ISBN: 978-1-998871-07-0

DAVID ARCHER
3420 AVENUE WILSON
SUITE 101
MONTREAL QC, CANADA, H4A-2T5

david@archertherapy.com
www.transformingcomplextrauma.com

David Archer is available to speak at your business or conference event on a variety of topics. Send an email to david@archertherapy.com for booking information.

ADVANCE PRAISE

"*Transforming Complex Trauma* summarizes Rhythm and Processing (RAP) psychotherapy and demonstrates the need for such an approach by detailing the context of racial and intersectional discrimination that so many racialized survivors of violence experience. By centering humanity and human dignity, Archer shares this book with gratitude, in which practicing clinicians, student clinicians, researchers, and/or racialized survivors can see ourselves and our roles in using anti-racism to transform this world—while collectively working towards healing ourselves, our communities, and each other."

—Jennifer M. Gómez, Ph.D.
Assistant Professor in the School of Social Work at Boston University
Board Member of the Center for Institutional Courage
Author of *The Cultural Betrayal of Black Women & Girls: A Black Feminist Approach to Healing from Sexual Abuse*

"David Archer provides a compelling anti-racist and culturally informed model for changing how mental health services are delivered. His sweeping work provides an entirely new model for conducting anti-racist psychotherapy in ways that are accessible to both therapists and clients."

—Thomas Zimmerman, Ms.Ed., LPCC
EMDRIA Approved Consultant, EMDR Therapy Trainer

"'The world needs to change.' Archer is clear that change in our society requires a metamorphosis that includes healing from within. By moving beyond blame and shame of individuals based on identity, Archer highlights ways to transform complex trauma in a way that centers hope for recovery. If you are a practitioner that has wanted to see that there are ways to be person centered, culturally responsive, and effective, this book is where Archer speaks truth to power and helps us see the possibility of true mental health transformation. This is a must read for practitioners in training and will be included in my future courses."

—Daicia Price, PhD, LMSW, QMHP, CMHP
Clinical Associate Professor of Social Work
Director of Diversity, Equity, and Inclusion
University of Michigan School of Social Work

"In this book, David Archer gracefully takes you on a journey through the lived experiences of racially marginalized folk (through an intersectional lens). You can feel his compassion and know-how as your worldview and practical lens are subtly challenged. This book is an important read as we shift into an era where we seek to heal the ever-present wounds of a racist past."

—Norissa Williams, PhD
Liberation Research & Practice Institute
Founder & CEO

"This groundbreaking text and its corresponding curriculum should be incorporated into every graduate program in our field…David Archer is a visionary for our times, a "revolutionary therapist" in the best sense. I am honored to learn from and be led by him."

—Gayle A. Cordes, MBA, MC, DBH
Graduate Faculty
Cummings Graduate Institute for Behavioral Health Studies
Trauma Subject Matter Expert

"Last summer I read, with pleasure and delight, his 2022 book *Racial Trauma Recovery: Healing our Past Using Rhythm and Processing*. But that is nothing compared to the pleasure and delight I now have in reading this culminating work! Let me shout out that now, I want to be a revolutionary therapist! Let me join the clarion call for all of us to become revolutionary therapists!

David writes beautifully, and in his own voice. He has thought deeply and brought the whole of his human experience to his work. It is personal, and it is profound. Every clinician should read this book. With it, we really can change, or in Francine Shapiro's words, 'reduce the cycle of violence' in the world."

— Barbara Horne MASc, RP, RMFT
EMDRIA-Approved Consultant & Trainer
Niagara Stress & Trauma Clinic
Director, NSTC's EMDR Training Programs

"David Archer's newest book, Transforming Complex Trauma: Reflections on Anti-Racist Psychotherapy, is a culmination of his extensive research and experience in the field, offering a unique and much-needed perspective on addressing the complexities of racial trauma.

One thing that sets this book apart is its focus on the Rhythm and Processing Strategies (RAP) technique. This innovative approach empowers therapists to effectively navigate the terrain of racial trauma with their clients. RAP allows clients to choose the emotional feeling they want to address, giving them agency and control over their healing process.

The genius of RAP lies in its focus on destabilizing and re-encoding traumatic memories. This is achieved through actions that directly contradict the deep-seated emotions associated with the trauma. By taking the opposite of what's deeply felt, or by engaging in general actions that shift the power dynamic, clients are able to rewrite their narratives and reclaim their sense of agency.

Here's what you can expect from this book:

- A comprehensive understanding of racial trauma and its impact on individuals and communities.
- A clear and concise explanation of the RAP technique and its application in therapy.
- Case studies that illustrate the effectiveness of RAP in real-world settings.
- Practical tools and exercises for therapists to integrate RAP into their practice.
- A deeper understanding of the intersection between race, trauma, and healing.

Whether you're a therapist, a client seeking healing, or simply someone interested in understanding the complexities of racial trauma, *Transforming Complex Trauma* is a must-read. It offers a powerful and transformative approach to healing, one that has the potential to revolutionize the field of mental health and create a more just and equitable society."

—Carol Miles, LCSW
EMDRIA Past President, EMDR Certified Therapist
EMDRIA Approved Consultant
EMDRIA Approved EMDR Therapy Trainer
2023 Outstanding Contribution to EMDRIA Award Winner

PREFACE

TO THE READER

My Gratitude to You

As I write this, knowing my words will reach you, whoever you are, I thank you. When I first began to develop an approach to therapy that could work better for both complex and racial trauma and to write and speak about it, I never imagined that my words would reach states, countries, and continents I have never been to. I hope my words can inspire you to realize your own dreams and help others in the process.

Our Ancient Mother

The story of humanity begins in Africa between 140,000 and 290,000 years ago. It starts with Mitochondrial Eve, the mother of our species. The ancient ancestor of all modern humans. Her dark skin glistened in the sunlight as she made her way through nature—she was what we would now call a Black woman. Although the origin of humanity caused a variety of emotional reactions among some scientists brought on by their own hang-ups,[1] it is reality. This means that everyone who will ever read this book can trace their genealogy to the same place as me. It means that we are all family.

There was no race at that time. Just people. There was no racial trauma, but there was most definitely suffering. There were no therapists, but Mitochondrial Eve found ways of coping before we ever started writing about it. Over time, she made sense of her natural environment and survived. The subsequent growth of her families, tribes, and communities brought new ways of healing into the world. These could have been ancient rituals, ceremonies, and mindfulness practices that are forever lost now. But I imagine that our unknown ancestors healed

---

[1] Oikkonen, V. (2015). Mitochondrial Eve and the affective politics of human ancestry: Winner of the 2015 Catharine Stimpson prize for outstanding feminist scholarship. *Signs: Journal of Women in Culture and Society*, 40(3), 747–772.

mainly through experience—not through some scientific theory, not by venting, but by an experiential process.

Whether it was by singing, with the drum, with water, with plant medicines, or even herbs and spices, we learned to heal. We found ways of living in harmony with nature. Someway and somehow, our unknown ancestors managed to survive, reproduce, and survive again. As is the nature of humanity, with our infinite creativity, we've always found ways to adapt. Hundreds of thousands of years later brought us to this very moment.

How I Got Here

My name is David Archer. I am a Black Jamaican African Canadian who lives in the city of Montreal. My first job is being a father. My second involves working in the field of mental health. I specialize in treating complex trauma and helping people heal from racial trauma. In searching for a way to help those of my clients who suffered from an unforgiving childhood, an environment of fear, and a hostile social hierarchy, I developed a method that gets great results when working with people who have seen some of the worst the world has to offer.

As a social worker in a large, multicultural city, I have heard some of the most tragic stories that the public will never learn about. I have seen both some of the most devastating effects of poverty and the regular everyday injustices that it brings to children and their families. I have seen, heard, and sat with the deepest of sadnesses.

As a couple and family therapist, I have seen some of the most beautiful people shed the ugliness of the violent relational patterns that we all learn based on the stories of our genders. I have seen people change themselves and their families for the better. I have laughed with, smiled at, and embraced the greatest of loves.

As a psychotherapist, I have read and studied as much as I could, seeking to find a way to help people heal from "treatment resistant" disorders. I've seen women crawl out from under the weight of addictions. I've watched as children shattered the crushing barriers of eating disorders. I've seen men learn to love themselves after their society told them every reason that they shouldn't.

I write this book because I have met people who gave up on their lives or had their lives taken from them, and I don't want that to happen anymore. I seek to eliminate suffering, to transmute it to wisdom, and to teach others to do the same thing.

Before treating trauma, I was a student counselor; before that, I was an English teacher for newcomers; even before that, I was a software engineer; and before all of the above, I was an artist. I am the sum of my experiences and the product of my environment—an environment where we were poor, but my parents still did the best that they could. In a political context where my province was in conflict with the rest of its country. In a colonial context where Indigenous people fought for self-determination. In this world where one's racial identification influences where they stand on these and many other issues. Out of this world, I exist.

The Drive for Anti-Racist Change

I am an anti-racist psychotherapist
because the world needs to change.

People use power to influence the lives of others, leaving traumatic histories in their wake. One of the greatest examples of this is the original sin of North America, rooted in European authority. In the 15th century, the Roman Catholic church created the Doctrine of Discovery[2] to

---

[2] Miller, R. J. (2019). The doctrine of discovery: The international law of colonialism. *Indigenous Peoples' JL Culture & Resistance, 5*(1), 35–42.

address the question of the Indigenous people who lived on the lands the Europeans coveted. Endorsed by European monarchies, this doctrine justified the colonization, brutalization, and enslavement of non-Christians for as long as the rulers deemed it necessary. This policy led to genocidal acts, settler colonialism, and mass displacement—a violence that ravaged the Western hemisphere. Although the violent creation of these nation-states did not originate from Christianity per se, it was used as a justification. Racism, like other "isms," serves to rationalize violence, greed, and domination.

My primary problem is with whiteness or, to be more specific, that which causes racism and other "isms" to exist. Whiteness can be understood as that which creates and maintains domination, "normality," and privilege[3]. The problem of whiteness does not refer to white *people* in particular but to ideas created hundreds of years ago to justify the oppression, colonization, and enslavement of non-white people. The social structure we operate in North America is based on dominance; its systems continue to uphold social, economic, cultural, and political structures that benefit the few at the expense of the many.

The primary motivation for the enslavement of my ancestors was not the evil of white *individuals* but the goal of creating a world where the elite could exploit poor laborers (as through the indentured servitude of "whites" and other people) and then exploit free labor (through the multigenerational, transnational violence of chattel slavery). You can't talk about race without talking about capitalism. The Trinidad and Tobago historian and statesman Eric Williams was a crucial voice who thoroughly explained this in his landmark book that is aptly named *Capitalism and Slavery*.[4] Being anti-racist involves critiquing the economic system that maintains oppression.

---

[3] Green, M. J., Sonn, C. C., & Matsebula, J. (2007). Reviewing whiteness: Theory, research, and possibilities. *South African Journal of Psychology, 37*(3), 389–419.

[4] Williams, E. (2021). *Capitalism and Slavery*. UNC Press Books.

For the reasons listed above, my anti-racism is intersectional. I cannot separate my anti-racism from the anti-colonialism of calling out the genocide and forced displacement of the Indigenous peoples of Turtle Island (i.e. North America), Palestine, or other colonized regions. My anti-racism is linked with the struggle for reproductive rights. In this way, it is linked with feminism. My approach is also anti-orientalist. We oppose the anti-Asian violence that has seen an uptick in recent years due to COVID conspiracies. We oppose Islamophobia and the anti-immigration policies aimed against Latino, Latina and Latinx people. These are all manifestations of the endless war against those who are oppressed.

As I write this, I realize that these were not problems that Mitochondrial Eve would have needed to deal with. We have developed technologies that protect us from many of the dangers Mitochondrial Eve faced from her natural environment, but we have created an unnatural, exploitative social structure that protects the interests of the few while bringing adversity and new dangers to the many, and especially to those that this structure, this whiteness, categorizes as "non-white."

Why Did I Write This Book?

Months before I decided to write this book, I was invited to present as a plenary speaker at the International Society for the Study of Trauma and Dissociation. There, I gave a case presentation on my anti-racist approach with a white Canadian woman, as well as a description of the theory that supports my results. I explained that gendered violence, violence against LGBTQ people, and racial trauma leads to dissociative symptoms, and I demonstrated how to reprocess traumatic events in a short video segment with a Black woman from the West Indies. The presentation was well received. Many people had never seen or heard of an approach like it before.

After receiving encouragement from members of the audience, I knew that more people needed to learn about this approach and its capacity to transform complex trauma symptoms. It is an approach that takes the identity of the individual into account as one of the fundamental cores of anti-racist psychotherapy, leading to lasting, transformative change. This is why I must share it with the world.

This book is meant to educate and inspire the next generation of revolutionary therapists. And what's a revolutionary therapist, you might ask? It's a person (from any discipline) who challenges traditional practices, advocates for transformative change, and serves those who are oppressed regardless of their social identity. We need different therapeutic approaches and we need different perspectives. We need a revolution in our practice.

Why Do We Need Something Different?

During my studies, before I trained in Eye Movement Desensitization and Reprocessing (EMDR) therapy,[5] before I gave any workshops or presentations, I did not find many approaches that spoke to what was important for me. I knew that I wanted to help people who were suffering, and I knew there was a way to help them. But the therapeutic approaches I studied did not always address the problems of the people I met with. Sure, some people just need someone to talk to about their problems, but others are looking for an actual solution to those problems. People need to know about their own cognitive distortions,[6] but many problems do not stem from a person's thought patterns alone. The scale of mental health issues in our society points to

---

[5] An evidenced-based psychotherapy treatment designed to treat distress related to traumatic memories.

[6] Biased beliefs and overgeneralizations about ourselves and the world around us; for example, black-and-white thinking or catastrophizing situations.

a common cause, at a higher level than just the individual, a common cause embedded in the structure of our society.

We need real change. We need something different from victim-blaming approaches. We need everyone to know they deserve to heal from their suffering. We need methods that take into account the unique identities of the client and therapist but that also address our common social context. We need something that can heal the wounds that we carry from the past. With so much going on in the world right now—warfare, pandemics, global climate crises—we need a new model of mental well-being. It is our responsibility to be cycle breakers; otherwise, we won't be able to manage when things get tougher. The future depends on it. Our ancestors have been waiting for it. So, let's get to it.

The purpose of this book is to inform the public about anti-racist psychotherapy, a trauma-based understanding of racial trauma. This book also hopes to explain the fundamentals of Rhythm and Processing Strategies, an integrative therapeutic framework to treat complex trauma and complex racial trauma symptoms. Combining the two, I hope we can heal in a way free of hierarchy, awaken ourselves from the cycles of suffering, and recognize that we have the technology to help people heal forever.

What to Expect

Reading this book should provide the basic information needed to understand racism from a trauma-informed lens, to understand complex trauma from a simplified perspective, and to learn a revolutionary way to help people of all backgrounds to recover from the suffering of their past.

This book is meant to summarize my lengthier books on *Anti-Racist Psychotherapy*,[7] *Black Meditation*,[8] and *Racial Trauma Recovery*,[9] so as to introduce my ideas to the largest possible audience. I also hope it will encourage interested readers to explore my ideas in more depth in those books.

The first three chapters of this book set the foundation. They explain what anti-racist psychotherapy is concerned with, the trauma-based understanding of anti-Black racism, and its intersection with complex trauma. Chapters five and six introduce the Africentric principles that underlie anti-racist psychotherapy and the concept of memory reconsolidation, which is integral to transformative change.

Chapters seven and eight discuss the Rhythm and Processing framework, including the cycle of consolidation, resources for bringing about change, and the RAP technique, an approach designed to revolutionize the treatment of complex racial trauma. The last chapter covers the limitations and possible critiques of my critical theories, addressing some concerns and questions related to anti-racism in the counseling domain that have come up over the years.

And so I offer these words in gratitude to you. To the therapist, I hope that you can also help others to experience the tearful joy and gratitude my clients experience. To the student-therapist, I hope you can also learn an approach that can inspire you and expand your own horizons. And to the trauma survivor, know that I too have struggled with a social structure that can be unforgiving. Just know that as I have recovered, and my clients have healed, know that you can too. Our ability to recover is a gift from our common ancestors; so from mitochondrial

---

[7] Archer, D. (2021). *Anti-racist psychotherapy: Confronting systemic racism and healing racial trauma.* Each One Teach One Publications.

[8] Archer, D. (2021). *Black meditation: Ten practices for self-care, mindfulness, and self-determination.* Each One Teach One Publications.

[9] Archer, D. (2022). *Racial trauma recovery: Healing our past using Rhythm and Processing.* Each One Teach One Publications.

cousin to cousin, I wish you all the best and hope this book can guide your growth. May these words inspire you. May we transform the suffering in our world and bring peace to all people, cultures, and communities.

TABLE OF CONTENTS

CHAPTER 1

※

MENTAL HEALTH METAMORPHOSIS

First Session

I remember the first time that I wanted to see a therapist. Part of it was because I wanted to know what it was like to be a client during my educational training—just to be in the same room as someone who would have been doing the work I'd wanted to do for years. I also wanted to see how my own problems could be solved by talking about them.

"What area?" Ever cheerful, the receptionist was trying to get me connected to a therapist from my insurance policy.

"Montreal," I responded.

"Is there a specific type of therapist you would be interested in?"

"Huh?"

"What type of therapy would you like?"

"I want something unconventional. Could I meet someone who does, I don't know, neurolinguistic programming or some kind of hypnosis?"

"O-Oh!" She sounded pleased. "Sure, we have a few of those. Anything else you are looking for in a therapist?"

"A therapist that's Black."

The line went silent.

"Oh." The receptionist sounded disappointed. Was she upset with me? The tone changed; she now huffed and puffed with her responses.

"Well! Fine!"

Yeah. She was taking this personally and became passive-aggressive for the rest of the call. This was years ago, and I still remember that feeling in the pit of my stomach, as if my request was *bad*. In the end, I actually was paired up with a Black therapist, but she was only available by phone since she lived outside of my province. At the time, she was one of the only few in the country who worked with that insurance company.

Although I was skeptical back then about using a therapy only available by telehealth, it was one of the best decisions of my life.

This highlighted how hard it was to find a therapist who had an unconventional approach, but it also let me know that while many people would have attempted to please this gatekeeper, I wasn't one of them.

Ever since I talked to a therapist who understood racial trauma, I've wanted to help others in the same way.

What Is Race?

First off, race is not real. Don't get me wrong; racial differences are real. Black women are more than three to four times as likely to have a pregnancy-related death than white women.[10] Hypersegregation (the conscious decision by white Americans to segregate themselves from other races) affects African Americans more than any other racial grouping in the United States.[11] Black youth are more likely to experience perceived racial discrimination, which leads to altered responses to stress in adulthood.[12] But race as an objective biological or scientific reality doesn't exist. Race is socially constructed, and as a social reality, it has

---

[10] Howell, E. A. (2018) Reducing disparities in severe maternal morbidity and mortality. *Clinical Obstetrics and Gynecology, 61*(2), 387–399.

[11] Massey, D. S. (2017a). Segregation and stratification: A biosocial perspective. In Beaver, K. M., and Walsh, A. (Eds.). *Biosocial Theories of Crime* (pp. 49–67). Routledge.

[12] Adam, E. K., Heissel, J. A., Zeiders, K. H., Richeson, J. A., Ross, E. C., Ehrlich, K. B., Levy, D., Kemeny, M., Brodish, A. B., Malanchuk, O., & Peck, S. C. (2015). Developmental histories of perceived racial discrimination and diurnal cortisol profiles in adulthood: A 20-year prospective study. *Psychoneuroendocrinology, 62*, 279–291.

very real effects and consequences. It's a made up concept, but we make it real when we favor one race over another.

Race has real consequences, as the studies cited above show, but it is not a biological or scientifically valid concept. Human life started in Africa. Doesn't matter what color you are or think you are. This means all people—you, your friends, your cousin's cousins—all of them are descended from the same common African ancestors. This is why race is a game that has been played on us. One of the primary motivations for racism was economic power; many Western countries were built on exploitation, cheap labor, and free labor. But there were other motivations as well. The concept of race was invented to differentiate, separate, and colonize people.

As I said, race is a social construction. What race means can be very different depending on what society you're a part of. If you are Black and have only been around Black people, race doesn't impact you the same way. Some Africans only become Black once they visit Canada. Some people only become Latino once they fly to the United States. We live in a system that categorizes us because of our labels.

When I am seen as a "Black" therapist, some people don't see it as a "real" therapist. If I am seen as a "Black" man, this is seen as different from just a "man." Black becomes a modifier that changes the word that follows it. A system that gives benefits based on imaginary labels is old-fashioned, outdated, and should be immediately dismantled.

What Is Trauma?

You hear a lot of people talk about trauma nowadays. Sometimes the term is overused, and sometimes it is minimized. My perspective is that certain events from the past can govern our lives, shape our beliefs, and change the course of our existence.

Trauma can be simply understood as either the presence of suffering or the absence of compassion. It is not only the bad thing that happens to you but also what happens when you are deprived of good things. Surviving violence can leave physical scars, but a child who is abandoned might suffer even more damage to their nervous system. It is all in how we interpret the story of our suffering. Not all traumas are the same, but there are two main categories.

The traumas that everyone knows about are the big, clear ones— Trauma with a capital "T." Like war, sexual violence, and car accidents. These are things that directly threaten the life or livelihood of the individual. They are generally recognized by our society as harmful, as clear threats to well-being, and things most people would find distressing.

Then there is the other category, what we would call small letter t-trauma. These events may not be life-threatening or externally severe from someone else's viewpoint. But even if not everyone sees them as big traumas, they can be just as upsetting for the person experiencing them. Like losing your wallet at eight years old, getting lost in a mall at three, or going through tough breakups as a young adult. There are many examples.

It doesn't matter if others think these events weren't traumatic; your nervous system makes the final call. The mind's perception of adversity creates adversity. Both the capital letter T and the small letter t can leave long-lasting psychological wounds. It's not about how anyone else thinks about it; it's about the pain that you feel from it.

What Is Racial Trauma?

Now, when we add "race" and "trauma" together, we get "racial trauma." One of the earliest mentions of "race-based traumatic stress"* in the scientific literature was by Robert T. Carter. This paper was published in 2007, showing that recognizing this kind of trauma is relatively new, even though racial trauma has a much longer history.[13]

Racial trauma generally refers to distressing events that are either real or perceived experiences of discrimination because of someone's race.[14] When we say "real or perceived" in racial trauma and anti-racist psychotherapy, it does not mean that the perceived event is not real. Instead, it's how the person interprets the event, regardless of anyone else's opinion, that defines its impact.

This means that our definition includes not only obvious acts of hatred or violence but also non-physical stressors. Being threatened, humiliated, or witnessing harm to others also qualify as race-based stresses. The authors explain that while African Americans often face these issues, Indigenous people, Asian Americans, and Latin Americans also go through hardships tied to their identities. Also keep in mind, we do not need to direct experience for it to qualify; witnessing or learning about other people's suffering can also cause what's known as "vicarious" trauma.

Some people experience traumatic events at a greater frequency and severity than others because of how society sees them. Pick any day and read the news. Some groups are targeted more than others because of how they look, what God they worship, or even what pronouns they use. This means that while some people gain privileges because of their

---

* Mental and emotional injuries due to racial discrimination, systemic racism, and hate crimes.

[13] Carter, R. T. (2007). Racism and psychological and emotional injury: Recognizing and assessing race-based traumatic stress. *The Counseling Psychologist, 35*(1), 13–105.

[14] Comas-Díaz, L., Hall, G. N., & Neville, H. A. (2019). Racial trauma: Theory, research, and healing: Introduction to the special issue. *American Psychologist, 74*(1), 1–5.

identities, others can get the short end of the stick. Considering all of the above, it's clear that people can be traumatized by the way others treat them based on their race.

Why Should I Care About Racial Trauma?

You don't need to care about racial trauma like I do. You don't need to care about how people heal or recover. My job is not to convince anyone or prove myself right. Not only is the science on my side explaining the differential impact of race in nearly all domains of life; not only has the extent of structural racism been studied and reiterated over the years, but I have also learned that it is wiser to speak to those who will listen than plead with fake friends or fair-weather allies.

There are many diversity, equity, and inclusion advocates who believe we must convince people to choose racial justice. But they've got the wrong focus. What they suggest is that racists should use nicer words because racially oppressed people are hurting. I'm different from that. We don't need conditional assistance. We don't need to plead for our humanity. We have no time to seek compassion from those who aren't naturally predisposed to giving it.

If George Floyd's murder didn't change your mind, if the United States' history of lynching and state-sanctioned violence didn't change your mind, if the continued oppression and increased racial violence in recent years didn't change your mind, then your brain is probably made of mayonnaise. I'm a therapist, not a doctor, but I would recommend getting that checked out.

Who Is This Book Primarily For?

Regardless of your color, this book is written for the next generation of therapists, badass activists, and people looking for an innovative theory for mental health recovery. It is for politically minded people who are interested in a book that cuts to the chase and want to know more about the philosophy of anti-racist psychotherapy, the adaptive information processing model* of EMDR therapy, the principles of memory reconsolidation,** and how fundamental Africentric principles*** work their way into the Rhythm and Processing therapy approach that I use with everyday people on a regular basis.

You can be of any race and benefit from this book, but my main focus is on the effects of anti-Black racism. There are many books that effectively discuss how racism affects Black individuals and other marginalized racial groups.[15] I focus more on Blackness because it has a special relationship to whiteness and the concept of there being an absolute good and an absolute evil in the world. But still, there are many ways to think about race or the idea of white insecurity/supremacy, and this book is just one of them.

Is Systemic Racism Linked to Mental Health?

In the many stories I have heard from trauma survivors over the years, I noticed that people's trauma histories depended on their identity. Not everyone experienced the same issues with discrimination, boundary violations, or workplace challenges. I had no choice but to think about

---

* The model suggests that mental health concerns arise from unprocessed memories due to distressing experiences; this forms the basis of EMDR therapy.

** The process of actively recalling previously constructed or consolidated memories so they can be reconsolidated—essential for therapy-induced transformative change.

*** Principles that highlight African cultural values and beliefs designed to promote psychological wellbeing in therapeutic contexts.

15 Acuña, R. (2000). *Occupied America: A history of Chicanos* (4th ed.). Pearson; Alexander, M. (2020). *The new Jim Crow: Mass incarceration in the age of colorblindness.* The New Press; Coates, T.-N. (2015). *Between the world and me.* Spiegel & Grau; Du Bois, W. E. B. (2017). *Black reconstruction in America: Toward a history of the part which Black folk played in the attempt to reconstruct democracy in America , 1860–1880.* Routledge; Takei, G., Eisinger, J., & Scott, S. (2019). *They called us enemy.* Top Shelf Productions; Said, E. W. (1979). *Orientalism.* Vintage; King, T. (2017). *The inconvenient Indian: A curious account of native people in North America .* Doubleday Canada.

how mental health tied in with how the person defined themselves in their own society.

Identity-based stresses led me to think about race-based stress, and then to look specifically at the effects of anti-Black racism. Because of my own personal experiences seeking therapy, as well as the clients who were seeking me out because they hadn't found any other anti-racist approaches, I also realized that not all therapists were thinking the same way about this.

While I was searching for a deeper way to understand the connections between race and mental health, I met with Dr. Heather Hall, a psychiatrist who has dedicated her career to understanding the implications of public health for trauma and dissociation. Her research on the interplay of race and mental health gives us insights that underlie many of the motivations for writing this book.

Dr. Hall's extensive review gives us five important findings:[16]

- **The Overdiagnosis of Schizophrenia:**
  - Minority groups are treated differently. Black Americans are diagnosed with schizophrenia more often than people in other groups.
- **Discrimination's Impact on Diagnosis:**
  - When Black Americans admit they have experienced discrimination because of their skin color, there is a higher likelihood that they will receive a schizophrenia diagnosis.
- **The Phenomenon of Social Defeat:**
  - There is a psychological impact from chronic experiences of discrimination, leading to a state called "social defeat." These repeated experiences lead to a loss of self-respect and group identity.

---

[16] Hall, H. (2022). Dissociation and misdiagnosis of schizophrenia in populations experiencing chronic discrimination and social defeat. *Journal of Trauma & Dissociation*, 1–15.

- **The Link Between Oppression and Internalized Shame:**
  - Experiencing oppression is related to the internalization of shame. Shame is a powerful emotion that drives dissociative symptoms and other mental health issues.
- **Chronic Shame and Mental Health:**
  - The persistent experience of shame, especially in relationship to anti-Black racism in our society, is a key driver in the development of complex mental health conditions.

The overdiagnosis of schizophrenia in Black communities is not an anomaly; it's a reflection of a deep-rooted systemic racism embedded in our healthcare system. The studies Dr. Hall cites support the view that the prejudice of the mental health practitioner can impact what should be objective, clinical assessments. Chronic discrimination is linked to social defeat, the internalization of shame, and the development of mental health conditions.

Beyond these important findings, Dr. Hall points out a significant gap in mental health care: the underassessment of complex PTSD and dissociative disorders, particularly in cases involving Black and other non-white people. At the same time, these very same mental health concerns are *highly* responsive to trauma-informed methods of treatment.

This speaks to why we need more trauma-informed—and especially racial-trauma–informed—approaches in mental health care. By learning to treat PTSD, complex trauma, and dissociative disorders, therapists can also become more effective at treating racial trauma. This book seeks to demonstrate that understanding racial trauma also better prepares us to transform complex trauma.

How Could This Benefit Society at Large?

Our society makes certain people more vulnerable than others. This is why racism is arguably one of the most challenging and problematic issues that we live with. But let's be clear: I am an intersectional anti-racist, meaning there are connections between our different oppressions. I have come to learn that racism is related to sexism. Racism is related to homophobia. Racism is related to capitalism.

The idea of classifying haves and have-nots, those who should rule and those who should follow, those who are more deserving of life and those who are not, also has to do with climate change. The most devastating effects of climate change hurt those who have the lowest incomes. And it doesn't stop there: those with lower incomes are generally women, people with disabilities, or other people who have been deprived of the privileges of a hierarchical society.

Taking this into account, racism, like sexism, ableism, and others, are only tools that create hierarchies and reinforce the larger economic system of capitalism, which also intersects with militarism. But don't get me started here. Just know that what I am writing is much bigger than just stopping rickety old racists on the internet from using slurs that they can't even spell properly.

Violence flourishes in a context that permits it. We don't eliminate racism without eliminating sexism. We don't eliminate xenophobia without eliminating the military-industrial complex. We call out antisemitism as much as we call out heterosexism. We don't get out of this unless we all get out of this. We can't leave anyone behind. When we learn that we can heal from complex racial trauma, we open our minds to the possibility that we can one day heal our society.

Summary

Racism is complex, but it is not permanent. We need an approach that is anti-oppressive because the world around us will only become increasingly diverse. Racial trauma has to be reckoned with. Because I've discovered efficient and effective methods to assist people with treatment-resistant issues, I know that with the right technology, we can heal this world. Racism was created, and as such, it can be destroyed. In fact, we have to destroy it. The world depends on it.

Just as finding the right therapist was important for me back then, I believe we all have a responsibility to help others to get the help they deserve. The next chapter will explain why embracing anti-racist psychotherapy and addressing scientific racism are essential steps not only for improving our practice of therapy but also for creating a more equitable society.

CHAPTER 2

RECOGNIZING RACISM IN SCIENCE

Seeing Your Reflection in Therapy

Ebony, a software engineer who spent much of her time surrounded by computers, never imagined she'd be sharing her own story during a video call. She was meeting with me online, away from the quiet aisles of her office cubicle. She was logical, straight-to-the point, and wanting something to change.

"How long have you had this anxiety?" I asked.

She sighed.

"It's been years, but I wasn't going to talk to just any therapist about it. Especially not a white therapist."

I used to be surprised by comments like these, but I've gotten used to it. But even if I thought I knew where she was coming from, I wanted her to tell me exactly what kept her from seeking help.

"I've been hearing that from other clients too, but what has been the main obstacle for you?"

"Generally"—Ebony looked off screen—"it's hard for me to open up. Some non-Black people are condescending. It's like they get pleased to hear you have problems."

Imagine that. She learnt not to share due to the possibility of encountering another professional's racism. She believed that even those who were supposed to help might secretly enjoy her suffering.

She went on to explain the reason for our meeting. Ebony found that when she was around people, she would feel intense judgment. She couldn't help it; she would suddenly shut down and stop talking.

"Can you explain more about how often this happens? Does it happen with friends?"

"No."

"Does it happen at work?"

"Yes, mostly."

"So, which types of people does this happen with the most?"

I asked the question, but I knew the answer. No wonder why Ebony couldn't meet with a white therapist. She literally wouldn't have been able to talk to them even in the session! Because of her internalization of racist judgments, she couldn't seek help. Because of the low number of Black therapists, she delayed seeking help. In some way, systemic racism reprogrammed her mind, so instead she learned to suffer in silence.

I have heard many stories like these over the years. The impact of racial discrimination is not always as straightforward as we think. There is a taboo to seeking mental health services in the Black community, but it does not come out of nowhere. My desire to change the way how mental health services are delivered grew even more after meeting people like Ebony.

The Need for Change

We need a revolution in therapy. Even though therapy on its own cannot resolve all the world's problems, it can address and alleviate individual mental burdens stemming from systemic problems such as racism. This chapter presents scientific evidence and scholarly references highlighting the need for an anti-racist approach to psychotherapy. I hope that after you read it, you will also understand on an intellectual level why we must transform our understanding of racism, comprehend the impact of scientific racism in our field, and acquire new perspectives for the twenty-first century.

The Persistence of Anti-Blackness

We have had years to reflect on the pandemic of anti-Black systemic racism. Online platforms are rife with hostile comments towards Black people, with a large amount of social media posts showing just that. Following George Floyd's murder in 2020, a study by Nguyen and their team [17] analyzed more than three million posts and noticed a brief drop in negative tweets about Black people, from 49.3% to 33.66%. But this improvement only lasted a few weeks before the negative views toward Black individuals went back to the usual level. This highlights the deep-rooted and persistent nature of racism across the United States. What is it that has driven anti-Black racism so deep in the American consciousness?

It wasn't just social media, either. In the three months after Floyd's murder, U.S. police killed over 300 individuals, with Black Americans making up 20% of the victims despite being only 13% of the population. This meant that racist police killings stayed constant, and in some cases even accelerated, despite global protests.[18] A 2023 report[19] revealed a staggering 35,000 law enforcement–related deaths since 2000, suggesting that the number of Black and Brown victims may be significantly underreported. African Americans, who constitute 12% of the U.S. population, account for 24.2% of police killings, while Latinos and white

---

[17] Nguyen, T. T., Criss, S., Michaels, E. K., Cross, R. I., Michaels, J. S., Dwivedi, P., Huang, D., Hsu, E., Mukhija, K., Nguyen, L. H., Yardi, I., Allen, A. M., Nguyen, Q. C. & Gee, G. C. (2021). Progress and push-back: How the killings of Ahmaud Arbery, Breonna Taylor, and George Floyd impacted public discourse on race and racism on Twitter. *SSM - Population Health*, 15, 100922.

[18] Cohen, L. (2020, September 10). It's been over 3 months since George Floyd was killed by police. Police are still killing Black people at disproportionate rates. https://www.cbsnews.com/news/george-floyd-killing-police-black-people-killed-164/

[19] La Raza Database Research Project. (2023). 2023 Final Report. https://www.csusb.edu/sites/default/files/RazaDatabase%20Report%20Final%20Version%2 0-min.pdf

people account for 19.5% and 48%, respectively. These statistics underscore the racial disparities in police violence.

Race impacts your chances of survival. But why is it that despite all of the protesting and calls for structural change, we still haven't been able to stop all of this violence?

Whitelash and the Response to Anti-Racism

Setbacks and whitelash responses against social justice are happening worldwide. My clients from different countries have shared their feelings of disappointment and betrayal. As I write this, the constitutional recognition of Indigenous people in Australia was rejected nationally and in every state. As I write this, bombs are being dropped on Palestine. Antisemitism and Islamophobia are seemingly at all-time highs in my country. Your race, indigenous status, and how the social structure shapes our identities can have an impact on what happens to you. This includes how you're treated on social media, your legal rights, and whether you're seen as having human rights.

The field of counseling and psychotherapy generally recognizes the problem of racism. In 2023, the American Counselling Association explained that racism is one of the biggest problems in society.[20] In 2021, the American Psychological Association apologized for the role of psychology in contributing to systemic racism in the United States.[21] The same year, the American Psychiatric Association apologized for its support for structural racism in the practice of psychiatry.[22] Following yet another widely publicized racist shooting in August 2023, the

---

[20] American Counseling Association. (2023). Anti-racism. https://www.counseling.org/knowledge-center/mental-health-resources/anti-racism

[21] American Psychological Association. (2021, October 29). Apology for systemic racism [press release]. https://www.apa.org/news/press/releases/2021/10/apology-systemic-racism

[22] American Psychiatric Association. (2021, January 18). APA apologizes for its support of racism in psychiatry [press release]. https://www.psychiatry.org/News-room/News-Releases/apa-apologizes-for-its-support-of-racism-in-psychi

American Psychological Association called for a renewed commitment to confronting racism and discrimination and addressing the needs of those most impacted.[23]

The mental health field generally supports anti-racism and is not, at the time of this writing, overtly against the concepts of critical race theory.[24] Still there is much more progress to be made because the problems are deeply embedded in the structure of our practice.

Structural Racism Within the Field

The importance of the apologies above and our ongoing progress becomes clear when we examine the challenges that are in our field. In a 2020 study, Dr. Monnica Williams, one of the world's foremost experts on racial microaggressions, explained that 53% of multi-ethnic clients report experiencing microaggressions from their therapists.[25] Additionally, most clinical training and academic curricula do not teach from an anti-racist perspective. This often leads to therapists having a preference for clients of their own race, poor outcomes for non-white

---

[23] American Psychological Association. (2023, August 29). Racially motivated shootings in Florida add to trauma, grief experienced by Black Americans, says APA president [press release]. https://www.apa.org/news/press/releases/2023/08/florida-racially-motivated-shootings

[24] Critical Race Theory was originally developed and popularized by the great legal scholar Derrick Bell. The theory explores the intersection of race and law to explain how systemic racism is ingrained in the legal system. To understand this theory, especially interest convergence—the idea that racial progress in the U.S. happens only when it suits the interests of white people—and its role in continuing racism in America, this article, as Bell describes it, is highly recommended:
Bell, D. A., Jr. (1980). Brown v. Board of Education and the interest-convergence dilemma. *Harvard Law Review*, 93(3), 518–533.

[25] Williams, M. T. (2020). *Managing microaggressions: Addressing everyday racism in therapeutic spaces*. Oxford Academic.

people in therapy, and a reluctance to discuss race-related topics or addressing one's own internalized racist beliefs.[26]

In a university counseling center, about half of the respondents who were racially or ethnically diverse reported experiencing microaggressions from their therapists.[27] Black clients are more likely to detect microaggressions in therapy, and the perception of them reduces the alliance with the therapist and any possibility of benefiting from sessions.[28]

Williams[29] lists four problems we must address to transform the discipline of psychology.

- **Insufficient psychologists of color**
  - Given the increases in Hispanic and African American populations in the United States, we need more.
- **Discrimination towards psychologists of color**
  - Decisions to award doctoral degrees favor white applicants, and non-white professors are usually given roles with less power and influence.
- **Anxiousness about discussing racism creates paralysis**
  - Taboos around discussing internalized anti-Black racism and/or white privilege feed into a lack of courage to create social change.

---

[26] Williams, M. T., Faber, S. C., & Duniya, C. (2022). Being an anti-racist clinician. *The Cognitive Behaviour Therapist*, 15, Article e19.

[27] Owen, J., Tao, K. W., Imel, Z. E., Wampold, B. E., & Rodolfa, E. (2014). Addressing racial and ethnic microaggressions in therapy. *Professional Psychology: Research and Practice, 45*(4), 283–290.

[28] DeAngelis, T. (2009). Unmasking 'racial micro aggressions.' *Monitor on Psychology, 40*(2), 42.

[29] Williams, M. T., Faber, S. C., & Duniya, C. (2022). Being an anti-racist clinician. *The Cognitive Behaviour Therapist*, 15, Article e19.

- **Students receive inadequate diversity education**
  - Newer generations of students are being taught multicultural counseling, but many older therapists have not received this training.

Racism in Our Scientific Roots

The debate over nature versus nurture goes way back to the times of Plato and Aristotle in the fourth century BCE. These philosophers are often viewed in Western culture as among the first to discuss whether we are primarily shaped by our inborn traits or the external environment. However, we must understand that they weren't the only people, nor the first to ever think about this. The profound knowledge of ancient Kemet (Egypt), which predates Greek philosophy, likely influenced their discussions.[*]

We know now that it's a mix of both; people are influenced by their inherited traits and their life experiences. But you will see that many prominent scientists and thinkers used to support a belief in biological determinism—the idea that all human behavior, thoughts, and actions are predetermined by genetics or other biological factors. What's interesting is that biological determinism gained popularity in Europe and North America during the nineteenth century, which was around the same time that scientific racism began to rear its ugly head.

---

[*] There's a wealth of evidence suggesting that Greek philosophers, including Socrates, Plato, and Aristotle, were influenced by ancient Egyptian science and philosophical ideas. See Anakwue, N. (2017). The African origins of Greek philosophy: Ancient Egypt in retrospect. *Phronimon*, 18, 167–180.

Blumenbach and the Creation of the Caucasian

In the nineteenth century, when Europe decided to divide up the world among itself, they looked to the previous century for justification. Johann Blumenbach, a German anatomist and one of the founders of what we would now call anthropology, is largely credited with coining the term "Caucasian" for white people in the late eighteenth century.

He decided on a Eurocentric origin for humanity, specifically in the Caucasus region. Although this was incorrect, he did not stop there. He also proclaimed that every other race was derived from Caucasians. Every other human was deemed as aesthetically degenerate, morally inferior, and intellectually lower compared to the original "ancestral white race."[30]

He did this because he liked the dimensions of the skulls of the people from the region and didn't like anyone else's. His personal preference had important consequences, no matter how ridiculous and pseudoscientific it sounds now. But: pseudoscientific? "Shmudoscientific," they said. The legal system of the newly independent United States drew on his terms and definitions to decide who could become citizens.

The term "Caucasian" has always been associated with racial hierarchy, leading some to argue that it should be discontinued in scientific texts.[31] We must really pause and think about why this term is still in use—oh yeah, I almost forgot: Racism.

---

[30] Fredrickson, G. M. (with Camarillo, A). (2015). *Racism: A short history*. Princeton University Press. (Original work published 2002)

[31] Mukhopadhyay, C. C. (2008). Getting rid of the word "Caucasian." In M. Pollack, (Ed.), *Everyday antiracism: Getting real about race in school* (pp. 12–16). The New Press.

Linnaeus and the Divisions of Humanity

Elsewhere, during the eighteenth century, the Swedish botanist, physician, and zoologist Carl Linnaeus came up with a convenient idea that could be used to support the "scientific" justifications for imperialism, colonization, and violence. Even though he was the first to coin the term *Homo sapiens*—and his classification system as applied to plants and animals is still the basis for a whole lot of biological theories and definitions—Linnaeus' 1735 *Systema Naturae*[32] divided all of us into four groups: "Europaeus albus" (white Europeans), "Americanus rubescens" (Red Americans), "Asiaticus fuscus" (Yellowish-Brownish Asians), and "Africanus niger" (Black Africans).

Not only did he give these physical descriptors, oversimplifications of large groups of people, but he also, of course, gave moral characteristics to them. Europaeus was "wise," Americanus was "obstinate," Asiaticus was "greedy," and Africanus was "lazy." Much of this was likely based on the stereotypes already common back in the day, and Linnaeus did nothing to challenge them. Theories like these contributed to beliefs in racial determinism, in which a person's race determined their behavioral characteristics, an idea designed to prop up the belief that white people were superior to others.

Gall and His Skulls

In the early nineteenth century, Franz Joseph Gall proposed a pseudoscientific theory called phrenology. The idea was that the shape of one's skull was a primary determinant of their cognitive abilities and potential. He believed the external skull could map the parts of the brain responsible for different mental functions. Although this was key to creating interest in neuroscience and psychological theories by making

---

[32] Linnaeus, C. (1964). *Systema Naturae* (10th ed., Vol. 45). J. Cramer; Stechert-Hafner Service Agency. (Original work published 1759).

associations and assisting our understanding of brain localization, it was, despite being debunked, also one of many "scientific" theories used to justify racial bias.

The Nazis used pseudo-scientific racist theories, including some aspects of phrenology, to justify the persecution of Jewish people and others in the 20th century. In a similar fashion, Belgian rule in Rwanda in the mid-twentieth century, first as a League of Nations mandate and then as a UN trust territory exacerbated ethnic hatred between Tutsi and Hutu, which fed into the conditions that incited the Rwandan genocide.[33] These are just some examples of how crimes against humanity can sometimes involve the use of distorted scientific ideas.[*]

Darwin and the Evolution of Racism

Charles Darwin published *The Origin of Species* in 1859. The theory of evolution was, to say the least, groundbreaking, and its impact was vast across different fields of thought. For this reason, we also needed to learn about him and his followers in my introductory psychology classes when I was doing my bachelor's degree. But as important as his contributions were, racism was still in style when he was writing them back then.

Although Darwin correctly classified humans as a single species, he still believed in racial hierarchies and saw "savages"—that is, non-whites—as less evolved than "civilized" people—that is, Europeans and their descendants. But it didn't stop there: not only did he believe that white races were more evolutionarily advanced than Black races but also that men were biologically superior to women. This latter point may have

---

[33] André, C. (2018). Phrenology and the Rwandan genocide. *Arquivos de neuro-psiquiatria, 76*, 277-282.

[*] Although this is not related to scientific racism, we have to mention the unspeakably brutal governance of the Belgian Congo, especially under the personal rule of King Leopold II (who is arguably the most disgustingly vile man to appear on this planet). I could not confirm whether he used the same pseudoscientific ideas, but it's important to mention this, because some of my clients were displaced from that region due to his atrocities.

been influenced by his cousin Francis Galton, who also believed that genius was inherited through the male line rather than the female line.[34] Darwin was interested in the ideas that Galton would later dub eugenics.

Eugenics and the Myth of Superiority

Eugenicists, who wanted only "superior" people to be able to reproduce, grew in prominence in the early twentieth century. Generally, they decided that there were subclasses of Caucasians, such as Nordics, Alpines, Mediterraneans, and Jews. Nordics were seen as intellectually superior to the other, lesser groups. Madison Grant was an American author who raised alarms about the pseudoscientific fears of race mixing and the need to preserve the "Nordic" race.

His work became influential and widespread, and his writings not only influenced the discriminatory Immigration Act of 1924 in the United States[35] but also helped inform Nazi philosophy and genocide— Hitler was said to consider Grant's book his "bible."[36] Similarly, it is important to note that the Nuremberg laws were influenced by the U.S. Jim Crow laws.[37] When the Nazis were developing their framework, they sought out evidence of similar ideas already in place. Their genocidal regime's racial ideology targeted people based on political classification, racism, ableism, heterosexism, and especially antisemitism.

---

[34] Rose, S. (2009). Darwin, race, and gender. *EMBO Reports, 10*(4), 297-298.

[35] Spiro, J. (2009). *Defending the Master Race: Conservation, eugenics, and the Legacy of Madison Grant.* University of Vermont Press.

[36] Weikart, R. (2004). *From Darwin to Hitler: Evolutionary ethics, eugenics, and racism in Germany.* Palgrave Macmillan.

[37] Whitman, J. Q. (2017). *Hitler's American model: The United States and the making of Nazi race law.* Princeton University Press.

The discrediting of Aryanism after the Holocaust, which resulted in the killing of millions, was a significant shift in Western racial ideology.[38] However, the evolution of the "white" identity among many Europeans and their transatlantic descendants was influenced by more than the scientific articles I have cited above.

During the 19th century, the United States' immigration policies were highly discriminatory, favoring immigrants from Northern and Western Europe while excluding groups such as Italians, Greeks, Poles, Russians, and Asians.[39] Similarly, England's brutal colonization of Ireland demonstrated that not all European ethnic groups were seen as white. However, having proximity to "whiteness" still led to completely different experiences than those of colonized non-white people.[40]

In any case, what is now seen as a unified category of white was once a collection of radically different, distinct types. Some Europeans were not even considered to possess the same level of whiteness over time. What is clear is that racial identity is often inconsistent and complex, and it is definitely not a fixed biological or even "scientific" concept, despite what anyone tries to tell you.

Consciously Choosing Social Justice

It is clear that some of the most influential scientific thinkers had political, or racist, motivations for their theories. This should impact how we teach and learn about the seminal works in our field. Science is not neutral, since it's carried out by imperfect humans who publish the research. But just pointing the finger at the examples above isn't enough.

---

[38] Zia-Ebrahimi, R. (2011). Self-orientalization and dislocation: The uses and abuses of the "Aryan" discourse in Iran. *Iranian Studies, 44*(4), 445–472.

[39] Cohn, D. (2015). *How U.S. immigration laws and rules have changed through history.* Pew Research Center. https://www.pewresearch.org/fact-tank/2015/09/30/how-u-s-immigration-laws-and-rules-have-changed-through-history/

[40] Peatling, G. K. (2005). The Whiteness of Ireland under and after the Union. *Journal of British Studies, 44*(1), 115–133.

We have to be self-reflective and take the mirror up to our own faces. Because we have all emerged out of the same society, we all have internalized aspects of anti-Black racism, sexism, heterosexism, and the other "isms." Being anti-racist is a conscious decision—one that we must actively choose every day.

Williams defines being an anti-racist as working to actively confront in-group preferences and discriminatory practices in the structure of our society. It involves taking actions with the goal of achieving equity for all, focusing on the voices of racially oppressed individuals, practicing cultural humility, being aware of our privileges, and striving to eliminate our biases.[41]

The reason why we need *anti-racist* psychotherapy is because this deep, bigoted behavior cannot be resolved at a purely cognitive level. As logical as their originators must have thought them to be, the pseudoscientific theories listed in the previous sections were used to justify the feelings and fears of their authors. Emotions are a big part of this. The problem of racism is also concerned with survival-based responses in our nervous system. This is true not only for the victims but also for the perpetrators, enablers, and bystanders who allow the trauma of racism to go unopposed.

White people also need to deal with racial trauma, but in very different ways. The experience of racial trauma that Black, Brown, and Indigenous people face arises in part from the anxiety that whiteness cultivates due to its inherent insecurity. Whiteness is constantly concerned with a fear of losing power or resources.

A person who hates Black people is not only consciously choosing to be racist but is driven to be so by a compulsion rooted in fear and faulty associations in their mind. A nearly involuntary association exists, just like it does for the trauma survivor who becomes hypervigilant after

---

[41] Williams, M. T., Faber, S. C., & Duniya, C. (2022). Being an anti-racist clinician. *The Cognitive Behaviour Therapist*, 15, Article e19.

seeing their trigger. You can attend as many courses and read as many books as you like, but the trauma of whiteness is multigenerational, reinforced by the environment, and re-created by the media. Just like an alcoholic damages his nervous system with drinking, the poison of racism corrodes our society, drowns our humanity, and is simply not meant for human consumption.

Addressing the Miseducation of the Therapist

We need to reflect on what we were taught. When people learn they no longer need to feed into old patterns, they have in some way re-educated themselves. The old pattern no longer triggers them, and a new way of looking at the world manifests. People around them notice. The trauma survivor changes from the inside out—new relationships, new boundaries, a whole new view of the future emerges. If such revolutionary changes can happen within an individual, then I believe the same can be done with the entire field.

To counter the effects of scientific racism and its impact on therapists and their clients, I have developed the Rhythm and Processing Strategies. More than a single technique, these strategies are a way of re-mixing all my previous psychotherapy training, linking it to a cohesive whole, and making it work for all of us. An approach to resolving the mental health consequences of racial trauma ended up being an approach that could also help people who suffer from complex trauma and other identity-based forms of stress. But it all started with listening to my clients and through critical self-reflection.

Summary

There is a need for anti-racist psychotherapy to confront the pervasive culture of systemic racism. Not only are there longstanding racial disparities in multiple healthcare domains, but there are also social inequalities that maintain cycles of discrimination. We have to confront the sickened roots of scientific racism; otherwise, it will keep producing bitter fruit that spreads into our psychotherapy and other domains. We need a revolutionary shift to a more empathic and effective paradigm. Rhythm and Processing Strategies are a promising way of achieving this.

We need to improve mental health outcomes across all racial, gender, and social identities, but we need self-reflection. We need to offer criticism where it is due and start off on the right foot. The next chapter will go over the basics of anti-racist psychotherapy, so we begin with the proper foundations. Let's transform our understanding. Let's transform complex trauma. And let's turn treatment-resistant mental health disorders into a forgotten memory of the past.

CHAPTER 3

INTERCONNECTIONS IN OUR SESSIONS

Righteous Anger

She looked at me from her screen, sitting and seething in her chair. Mariana was an Afro-Cuban navigating the turbulent waters of a male-dominated workplace. She came to see me because of the stress in her relationship and a society that tried to take her voice away.

"I think I've got some anger issues," Mariana said.

"Who do you get angry at?" I asked.

"That's the thing… I don't show it to anyone!"

Mariana's story was a common one. At work, she was told she was too sensitive, and at home, her boyfriend said she was too much. She was caught in a crossfire of other people's expectations. And if she tried to set boundaries, she became the one to blame.

"I just find myself getting so angry, and I'm like no, stop it."

"Why 'stop it'?"

"Huh?"

"Anger is not the problem in this situation."

"Really?"

I knew that she would be surprised to hear this. She thought that she was not supposed to be angry. But who taught her that? She suffered intrusive thoughts and so much self-judgment, but how many people took advantage of her because she didn't show her anger?

"Let's take a look at it this way: who benefits most from you not being angry?"

"Hmm… I never thought of it."

"Women are told they are not supposed to be angry so that the men in power can get away with anything they want. If oppressed people really got angry, they might use that anger to actually change things."

Mariana looked at me and paused.

"No one has ever told me that before."

The goal is for people to be fully human, not to cut them off from their emotions. At that point, we hadn't even started discussing the trauma. Instead, we focused on validating her side of the story, listing the downsides of the status quo, and understanding the benefit of each of her emotions. This shifted the entire purpose of our meetings.

There is no such thing as neutrality, and the therapist must take a side. In this case, I took the client's side. There were events that taught her to swallow her anger. There were men who benefitted from her submission. There were social norms that set the stage for all of this.

We found ways of healing from the events that set this in motion. She learned to reframe her emotions and own her assertiveness. And to her surprise, as she changed herself, her relationship to others improved too.

What Are the Basics of Anti-Racist Psychotherapy?

I'm the author of *Anti-Racist Psychotherapy*, but I am not the only anti-racist psychotherapist out there. Many authors have explained in their own ways how to do this work.[42] I stand on the shoulders of my

---

[42] Welsing, F. C. (1991). *The Isis (Yssis) papers.* Third World Press; Fanon, F. (1966). *The wretched of the Earth.* Grove Press; DeGruy-Leary, J. (2017). *Post-traumatic slave syndrome: America's legacy of enduring injury.* Joy DeGruy Publications Inc.; Menakem, R. (2021). *My grandmother's hands: Racialized trauma and the pathway to mending our hearts and bodies.* Penguin; Williams, M. T., Holmes,

ancestors in creating a new framework to address this old problem. The basic idea of anti-racist psychotherapy is that it is a trauma-informed exploration of anti-Black racism.

Through my practice, I have discovered ways of helping marginalized people facing a variety of mental health stresses, especially complex trauma symptoms. When I considered their relationships with those around them and their society, something different happened. I have witnessed many people's lives change before my eyes, and I feel a duty to share what I have learnt. Let's start with the four core ideas of anti-racist psychotherapy in general before moving on to the specifics.

The Four Cores of Anti-Racist Psychotherapy

All people exist in relationship to one another. We all know the expression that no man is an island. This is a good way of looking at it. Because even islands exist in relationship to what is around them. The island does not exist without water. The island is made up of earth, sand, or whatever makes up the ground, and these always form a collective.

We exist in relationship to other people, but also in relationship to what is important to us. We have our bodies, but what's also important is our beliefs, dreams, and how we define our life's purpose. These parts of our mind can be impacted by our experiences. Some of these experiences can keep us down like gravity, acting on us even if we don't see them. Keeping us from rising up or making healthy connections that can sustain us. We must shine the light on these forces. The four cores can help us to do this.

S., Zare, M., Haeny, A., & Faber, S. (2022). An evidence-based approach for treating stress and trauma due to racism. *Cognitive and Behavioral Practice, 30*(4), 565–588.

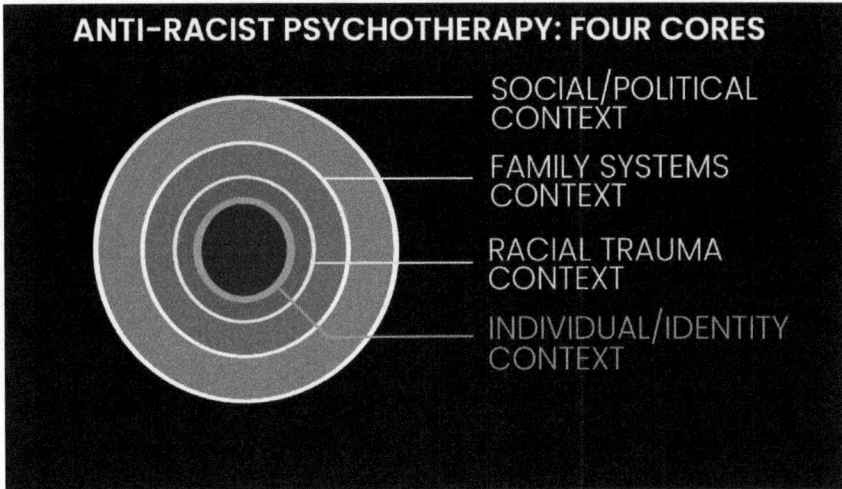

ANTI-RACIST PSYCHOTHERAPY: FOUR CORES

SOCIAL/POLITICAL CONTEXT

FAMILY SYSTEMS CONTEXT

RACIAL TRAUMA CONTEXT

INDIVIDUAL/IDENTITY CONTEXT

Social/Political Context

The social/political context surrounds us at a distance yet plays a vital role in our lives. It sets the standards for what we are meant to see as acceptable, what laws we follow, and who dictates our beliefs and behavior. This refers to more than your local government but the entire political and social structure of a society. It includes how these distant forces impact you, whether you like it or not.

An awareness of this context is essential in anti-racist psychotherapy. How we see ourselves as Black people is important, of course, but understanding how society sees us and why is equally important. If you meet a racist police officer, for example, whether you believe you are Black is beside the point; if *he* sees you as Black, he will treat you in whatever way he has been conditioned to believe a Black person should be treated.

If you are a citizen of a country that is seen as "Black," your passport may not always give you the same privileges as citizens from a different country. If you got to this chapter, then you probably already know all of this, but it remains to be said. It's how your identity is constructed outside of yourself.

The Family Systems Context

This is about more than your family; it relates to how you interact with others and how others interact with you. This context is related to family systems theory, which explains the name. These perspectives helped to inform my training as a couple and family therapist, and some aspects of it are essential for trauma treatment as well.

- **Homeostasis**
  - All systems seek to maintain and preserve equilibrium. Even if it is not beneficial for all members, a system will seek to maintain balance.
  - Conflicts can potentially destabilize a system. If this happens, the system will attempt to return to balance. Patterns of behavior naturally become stable over time.

- **Symptoms**
  - There is a function to any identified problem. Symptoms occur in response to a system that either maintains or, in some cases, benefits from them.
  - In family therapy, clinical experience has shown that whenever a child is presented as being the only symptomatic family member or the "identified patient," we must bring all members of the family into the room.
  - In some cases, the child's outbursts at school can *conveniently* distract the entire family from problems in the parents' marriage.
  - At a societal scale, we blame individuals for poverty but not a system that is skewed to favor the rich over the poor. In a therapeutic context, beliefs and actions originating from a person's trauma history influence their behavior and external relationships.
  - These beliefs also *conveniently* prevent or discourage confronting the oppressor that caused the trauma or the system that maintains the status quo in the first place.

- **Communication**
  - There are two layers to communication: the content and the implications.
  - Although we communicate using speech, tonality, or body language on a regular basis, some people can use it to reinforce their beliefs about who is in charge. They can use passive aggressiveness, scoffing, subtle slights, or even eye contact.
  - Our experiences inform how we communicate and how we interpret this communication.
- **Bi-directionality**
  - A can influence B, but B can also influence A. It is not only how someone communicates with you but also the way you receive it that ultimately determines the message of the communication.
  - This is helpful because it means we can actually challenge bad behavior and change how the world operates—but of course, only when we have the courage and the resources to do so.

As people heal and recover from trauma, their beliefs about their external relationships change. On a deeper level, they also change how they communicate with the inner, most vulnerable parts of themselves. We respect ourselves from the inside out. As we heal, we become better able to set boundaries and advocate for ourselves, as well as to communicate with integrity. The family systems context helps us to recognize how we impact and have become impacted by the people around us.

The Racial Trauma Context

This layer involves identity and trauma. When talking about trauma, the word race is usually left out except when we are speaking about non-white people. In this specific context, race is much more than that. I'm referring to the socially constructed identity of the individual. People experience a range of events, from subjective small-t trauma to objective capital-T trauma. These events happen to some people more often than others because of how our society categorizes us. Race is one of the best examples, so here it is a catch-all term for these socially constructed categorizations.

However, even though our identities are socially constructed, these events can still have real consequences. Many mental and physical health problems stem from stressful events in childhood. This is because when we accumulate trauma over time, due to their accumulation—being repetitive or chronic—and when it happens at pivotal moments in our development, it sets the groundwork for health problems that can last years, decades or even longer, their timing occurring during important developmental stages of people's lives.[43]

Some people experience stress from their environments that others do not. When we go through enough of these stresses, there is a "weathering" effect that leads to multiple biological dysregulations as the body repeatedly shifts in and out of homeostasis. This is part of what makes trauma survivors more vulnerable to physical and mental health issues than others. Regularly going through intense, survival-based responses leads us to create associations in our minds, which then creates the ideal conditions ripe for mental health problems.

But there is an upside. These problems are not permanent! Once we recognize that the mind and body are connected to what has happened to us, we can use that to our advantage. We can create experiences that can be used to repair the damage. Once we are conscious of what has harmed us because of who we are, and once we change the way how we have stored these memories, we can learn to appreciate ourselves for

---

[43] Shonkoff, J. P., Boyce, W. T., & McEwen, B. S. (2009). Neuroscience, molecular biology, and the childhood roots of health disparities: Building a new framework for health promotion and disease prevention. *JAMA, 301*(21), 2252–2259.

what we have overcome. This will be explored in the later chapters of this book.

Individual/Identity Context

The individual/identity context is where the transformation happens. The other layers are not under our direct control. We can't control what a politician will say, we can't stop coworkers from gossiping, and we can't prevent trauma from being traumatizing. But we can always change our beliefs. We can always learn new perspectives. And when we make changes internally, we can cause ripple effects in the world around us.

The individual/identity context represents the infinite creativity of the human mind. In this context we can find mindfulness, meditation practices, visualizations, and even our capacity to dream. Some people think that the therapist is responsible for healing, but I disagree. I'm only there to witness it. The therapist's responsibility is to make space for the client to recover their gifts.

From time to time, we need a break. We are constantly being judged by other people or even ourselves. When we have enough time to sit and focus, without all of the noise, expectations, and narratives, we can learn new things about ourselves. We can identify problems, visualize solutions, and think of new ways to be in the world. It is from this context that you have chosen to read this book. Your decision to follow each word, to absorb wisdom and to apply it—this is the context where life happens.

Racial Trauma and the Brain

At a basic level, racial trauma is defined as real or perceived experiences of racial discrimination.[44] Although that definition is helpful,

---

[44] Comas-Díaz et al., Racial trauma.

I have identified some other important considerations that are helpful for treating it. Let's start first with the neurobiological components.

The body responds to psychosocial stresses. The Sympathetic-Adrenal-Medullary (SAM) and Hypothalamic-Pituitary-Adrenal (HPA) axes are major parts of our body's stress response system.[45] Ongoing stresses can cause both of these axes to malfunction,[46] producing a range of problems. Whenever we encounter stresses, these systems help us react and respond.

Racial microaggressions at the supermarket, facing the glass ceiling in the workplace, stress in interpersonal relationships—these can all have real consequences on a person's nervous system. McEwen[47] explains that chronic stress leads to impairments in three main areas of the brain:

1. **Hippocampus:** The memory manager. Chronic stress causes it to malfunction, making it harder for us to accurately access memories.
2. **Amygdala:** Emotional response and threat detector. Chronic stress affects it by making our threat-detection system go haywire.
3. **Frontal Lobe:** The self-regulator. Chronic stress disrupts its functioning, which gets in the way of managing our actions, emotions, and behavior.

---

[45] Bierhaus, A., Wolf, J., Andrassy, M., Rohleder, N., Humpert, P. M., Petrov, D., Ferstl, R., von Eynatten, M., Wendt, T., Rudofsky, G., Joswig, M., Morcos, M., Schwaninger, M., McEwen, B., Kirschbaum, C., & Nawroth, P. P. (2003). A mechanism converting psychosocial stress into mononuclear cell activation. *Proceedings of the National Academy of Sciences of the United States of America*, 100(4), 1920–1925

[46] Michopoulos, V., Powers, A., Gillespie, C. F., Ressler, K. J., & Jovanovic, T. (2017). Inflammation in fear- and anxiety-based disorders: PTSD, GAD, and beyond. *Neuropsychopharmacology*, 42(1), 254-270.

[47] McEwen, B. S. (2006). Protective and damaging effects of stress mediators: Central role of the brain. *Dialogues in Clinical Neuroscience*, 8(4), 367–381.

The stress response system plays a key role in racial trauma. This is what makes our experience of these chronic stresses so confusing and even hard to describe. In fact, chronic stress changes the densities of some of these brain structures, so don't let anyone tell you that racism is harmless or just in your head. It actually affects the physical structure of your brain.

Understanding this neurological component, we can now dive into anti-racist psychotherapy's additions to the standard definition of racial trauma. The anti-racist perspective expands the experience of racial trauma into three dimensions—the multigenerational legacy, present-day oppression, and the social acceptance of suffering.

Multigenerational Legacy

The impact of our wounds goes beyond the individual. As Yehuda and colleagues[48] and Perroud and colleagues[49] showed, people who survived intense, traumatizing environments, such as the Holocaust and the Rwandan genocide, could pass on HPA axis alterations and mental health vulnerabilities to their descendants. This can happen while a mother is pregnant and directly exposed to trauma or even due to pre-conception stresses. In simple terms, we can inherit the trauma of our ancestors.

Let's pause and reflect on this. When a pregnant mother becomes traumatized, the surge of cortisol and the alterations to her stress response system not only affect her body but could also impact her baby. What if she carries a female fetus? Since girls are born with all the eggs

[48] Yehuda, R., Daskalakis, N. P., Bierer, L. M., Bader, H. N., Klengel, T., Holsboer, F., & Binder, E. B. (2016). Holocaust exposure induced intergenerational effects on FKBP5 methylation. *Biological Psychiatry, 80*(5), 372–380.

[49] Perroud, N., Rutembesa, E., Paoloni-Giacobino, A., Mutabaruka, J., Mutesa, L., Stenz, L., Malafosse, A., & Karege, F. (2014). The Tutsi genocide and transgenerational transmission of maternal stress: epigenetics and biology of the HPA axis. *The World Journal of Biological Psychiatry, 15*(4), 334–345.

they will carry in their lifetimes, the mother's trauma could even leave a mark on her grandchildren. This means that the wounds of the present can even scar the generations of tomorrow.

But I still have to mention, although this process of transmitting trauma between generations has some scientific support, we still need further studies to fully understand how and why this happens.[50] The studies I'm mentioning are all important, but they are limited to measuring events in our recent history. We still do not know the full impact of inherited trauma in African diasporic communities.

It's possible that our ancestors' experiences of physical, emotional, and psychological violence could have left echoes of mental health vulnerabilities. But trauma is only one side of the coin; on the flipside, our ancestors' will and resilience are why we are here today. We may have inherited suffering but the potential for wisdom also follows because mental health vulnerabilities are not immutable destinies. We are all descendants of unknown ancestors and unnamed heroes.

Contribution of Present-Day Oppression

Racial trauma is linked with alterations in cortisol, a hormone controlled by the HPA Axis and linked to stress.[51] When thinking about social stressors, there can be many culprits. Present-day oppression can affect us through discriminatory laws, exposure to stereotypes in media, and interpersonal microaggressions that our nervous system registers as dangerous, stressful, and even overwhelming. Remember, the stress response system does not distinguish between real and perceived dangers.

---

[50] Grasser, L. R., & Jovanovic, T. (2022). Neural impacts of stigma, racism, and discrimination. *Biological Psychiatry: Cognitive Neuroscience and Neuroimaging, 7*(12), 1225–1234.

[51] Harnett, N. G. (2020). Neurobiological consequences of racial disparities and environmental risks: A critical gap in understanding psychiatric disorders. *Neuropsychopharmacology, 45*(8), 1247–1250.

It does not matter if Becky said it was just a joke when she touched your hair or if Karen didn't mean harm by calling the police on your barbecue. Microaggressions can still be stress-inducing. Many people classify racist microaggressions as occurring due to unconscious bias. That's both an excuse and a misconception that I want to take my time with taking apart.

I have given presentations to corporations about the impact of microaggressions in the workplace. Not only are there multiple categories of racial microaggression to deal with,[52] but there are also gendered microaggressions for women in STEM fields.[53] Because of the breadth of these types of microaggressions, they can't all be "harmless." During these presentations, some attendees were shocked to see the big costs to these subtle slights. It's not just at the interpersonal level either; gender discrimination hurts the entire economy.

Calvalcanti and Tavares[54] explain, for example, that if the United States assumed the same level of gender inequality for wages that Egypt has, their output per capita would be reduced by more than half. However, their output per capita would increase by 17% if they reduced their gender inequality to the levels that Sweden has. If that wasn't convincing enough, their jaws dropped once they saw the amount of headlines showing the many millions companies owed due to gender discrimination lawsuits.

Gender discrimination can psychologically damage employees as well as critically damage any company's wallet once the lawyers come into the picture. Nobody wins. There is a significant financial cost to

[52] Williams, M. T., Skinta, M. D., & Martin-Willett, R. (2021). After Pierce and Sue: A revised racial microaggressions taxonomy. *Perspectives on Psychological Science, 16*(5), 991–1007.

[53] Kim, J. Y., & Meister, A. (2023). Microaggressions, interrupted: The experience and effects of gender microaggressions for women in STEM. *Journal of Business Ethics, 185*(3), 513–531.

[54] Cavalcanti, T., & Tavares, J. (2016). The output cost of gender discrimination: A model-based macroeconomics estimate. *The Economic Journal, 126*(590), 109–134.

companies, universities, and other large-scale organizations when they don't take these issues seriously.

Microaggressions carry both an effect and a function. Microaggressions, regardless of the stated assumptions and motivations behind them, maintain and benefit hierarchies and privilege. They fuel and re-create stereotypes and disparities. Because they happen so often to many of my clients, they are not even a personal thing; it is simply that power has no choice but to create and re-create victims from its existence. Although people with privilege might not consciously realize what they are doing, some studies show that people with more aggressive traits end up using microaggressions more than others.

But let's keep in mind, this is not a permanent problem that occurs in white people towards non-white or men toward women. It's also not some completely unconscious action, otherwise it would be both undetectable and unchangeable. With enough motivation, people can reduce microaggressions, improve prosocial behavior, and change their beliefs about people who are different.[55]

Social Acceptance of Suffering

It's sad to say, but there's a level of suffering that must be reached before people become outraged. Colonization can be a delicate topic. Non-Indigenous people distance themselves from the emotional gravity of it. They have their reasons. Maybe it is because we know that the forced relocations, land theft, and policies meant to attack Indigenous people make it easier to call ourselves North American. These made up thresholds for tolerating suffering are what allow genocides to happen.

---

[55] Williams, M. T., Kanter, J. W., Peña, A., Ching, T. H., & Oshin, L. (2020). Reducing microaggressions and promoting interracial connection: The racial harmony workshop. *Journal of Contextual Behavioral Science, 16,* 153–161.

We tolerate different levels of suffering depending on who the victims are, what they look like, and how far away they live from us.

Do we let this stuff slide because it means we get to keep our fancy smartphones and gadgets? In the West, violence directed at people near us or who look like us elicits a strong response (see the war in Ukraine), but there is often radio silence about the ongoing oppression of people we see as culturally or racially different (as seen in Palestine, Sudan, the Democratic Republic of Congo, Ethiopia, Yemen, and many other places). But once again, this extends beyond race or nationality.

I could go on, but the point is that some forms of violence are acceptable or not to be discussed. An important characteristic of racial trauma is that some people will not consider it to be trauma or even worth addressing. This is why organizing is essential. Without action through activism, protests, or consciousness-raising, the status quo cannot be challenged. Knowledge is power. Educating the public encourages others to think, to empathize, and to speak out for our common humanity.

Summary

Anti-racist psychotherapy's multi-dimensional perspective allows us to see that trauma, especially racial trauma, is much more commonplace than many of us realize. Who among us has not experienced undesirable events or been denied compassion in times of need? Treating this kind of difficulty requires us to understand the levels at which it exists. We have to consider social/political, family systems, racial trauma, and individual/identity contexts if we are to take an anti-racist perspective.

What *we* consider trauma is not important. What matters is the impact it has on the trauma survivor, which involves the transgenerational epigenetic inheritance of suffering, the activation and reactivation of oppression through microaggressions, and the social acceptance of suffering. Knowing all of this puts us in a better position to help people who have been traumatized because of their race, gender, or any other socially constructed identity.

Not all emotions are bad. In fact, our emotions can be our greatest teachers. But there are sometimes when the lessons are overwhelming. Next, we will dive deeper into the cycle that maintains these socially constructed experiences of suffering, as well as the function of betrayal at the individual, cultural, and institutional levels.

CHAPTER 4

TRAUMATIZATION AND DISSOCIATION

Taking Beliefs That Aren't Ours

The name Jasmine appeared on the bottom left of my screen. She was a dedicated professional and a child of Chinese and Haitian immigrants. It took a while before she was comfortable in our sessions. She was much more used to living in auto-pilot, always being on the go just to survive the dizzying pace of her workplace.

She looked at me through the screen of her smartphone. Becoming more experienced in my practice, I knew this was the point where we had to talk about more than just the dark under-eye circles showing her exhaustion. We had to go deeper, to unravel the beliefs that threatened to push her toward burnout.

"This job is killing me," Jasmine said.

"That's a problem. We need you to be alive to continue our sessions."

"Well, what do you want me to do? Quit?" Her voice quivered.

"Why not?"

"The money—how am I supposed to afford rent? How am I supposed to afford food?" She raised an eyebrow with a hint of sarcasm. "Besides, therapy isn't cheap, you know!"

"Of course." I smiled. "But I mean something a little different. What makes you think you can't find another job?"

We spoke about her accolades, her accomplishments in her job, and the fact that if she left, they would probably need two employees to replace her. But she was burning out. She was losing track of time, feeling like she was living in a fog.

"My friends think I'm doing *so* well, but I don't always believe them."

"Maybe it's because your workplace has convinced you that you're something that you're not."

We spoke about the microaggressions. We spoke about race in the workplace and how none of the people she saw getting raises looked like her. Even the white women, who had started their jobs after she had, flew past her with promotions.

"There were so many traumas that accumulated that you started to believe them." I said. "The belief that you are not good enough was completely made up. How else would you be able to do the work of two people?"

Tears welled up in her eyes. We were digging, and we struck something. But we needed more than just realizations. The constant betrayals, the lack of support—not only were they hurting her mentally, but she was feeling beaten down in her body. All of this was happening to the benefit of the workplace bullies and at the expense of the company's best workers.

Let's reflect on some questions:

- What is it that drives anti-Black racism and other forms of oppression?
- How can we make it so that marginalized people get better results from therapy?
- Can the same principles also improve therapy for all people?

To answer these questions, we need to start from an understanding of the binary complex trauma cycle.

The Binary Complex Trauma Cycle

The binary complex trauma cycle explains how oppressors distance themselves from negative traits while associating them to oppressed people. It also explains why the cycle is so frustratingly difficult to break. Racists usually don't admit to being racist, and they usually deny systemic racism. Liberal-minded people may believe that racism exists in our society but have great difficulty acknowledging their own racist beliefs. Regardless of your political affiliation, oppression is so much easier to point out whenever it's coming from someone else's political party.

Many people see Western media as becoming more "inclusive." Superhero movies are starting to be more diverse. Concepts like *white extremism* and *systemic racism* can be mentioned on air without too much pushback.* But the same coverage that highlights the power structure sometimes ends up reinforcing it. Some gains have been made, but in the lives of my clients, it does not always feel like there are tangible effects trickling down to their workplaces. Why are these problems so resistant to change? I will attempt to answer this from a racial-trauma-informed perspective.

We will examine the complexities of betrayal and why trauma that is interpersonal, cultural, and institutional carries a greater burden than other types. To do this, we need to take a deeper dive into our definitions. What is PTSD, what is complex trauma, and why does the word dissociation keep popping up throughout this book? I'll do my best to answer these questions and more so we can get to the bottom of what the binary complex trauma cycle is all about.

---

* With the exception of social media comments, "anti-woke" governors, white nationalist lobbyists, racist lawmakers, terrible comedians, etc.

PTSD and Complex PTSD

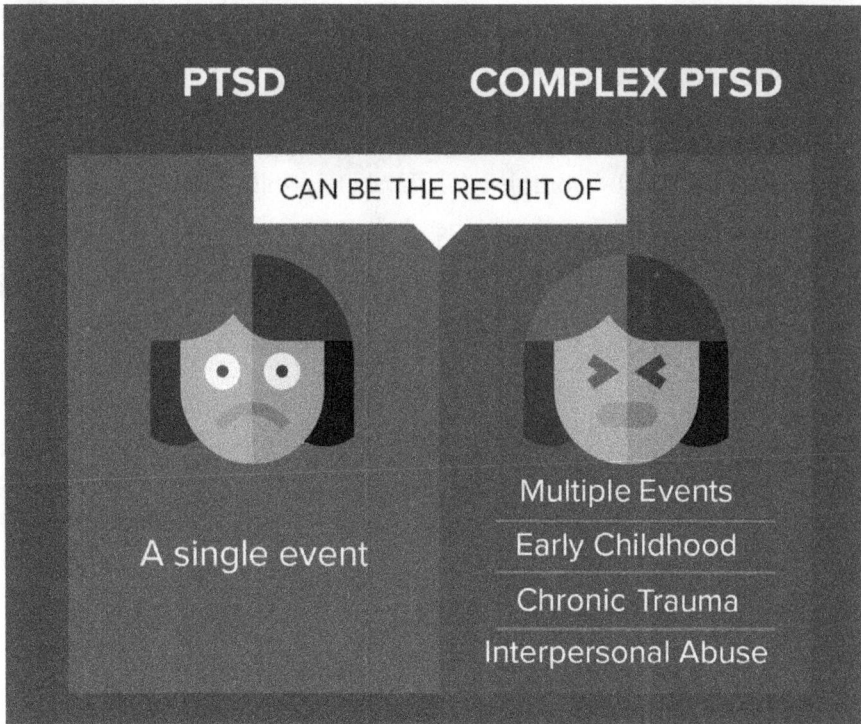

Image From: *Anti-Racist Psychotherapy*

The Post Traumatic Stress Disorder (PTSD) diagnosis requires specific criteria. Typically, these trauma sufferers experience intrusions (intrusive thoughts, nightmares), avoidance (doing what they can to avoid reminders of trauma), hypervigilance (being on the constant lookout for threats), and changes to self-concept because of trauma (changing one's thoughts or beliefs about oneself or one's relationships).[56]

Not all trauma is the same, and not all survivors have the same symptoms. Trauma happens across a spectrum. Also, most trauma survivors struggle with more than one traumatic experience. They usually

---

[56] American Psychiatric Association. (2013). *Diagnostic and statistical manual of mental disorders (DSM-5)*. American Psychiatric Pub.

meet with me because of multiple anxieties, phobias, and relationship problems. More often than not, I rarely meet people who have the "simple" form of PTSD. Instead, many of my clients have symptoms that look like complex trauma.

Dr. Judith Lewis Herman's groundbreaking 1992 paper gives an excellent definition of complex PTSD that is still relevant today. Her work can help to shed light on the challenges of complex trauma and what survivors struggle with.[57]

- **Repeated and Prolonged Trauma**
  - This includes going through experiences of abuse, captivity, or exposure to life-threatening situations.
- **Extended Impact on the Individual**
  - Beyond the core symptoms of PTSD, individuals can develop maladaptive beliefs about their perpetrators, such as taking perspectives like "I deserved it" or "they were justified in their actions."
- **Disruptions in Relationships and Identity**
  - People who have complex trauma struggle with keeping and maintaining relationships. Their lives become dominated by trust issues, feelings of alienation and helplessness.
- **Somatization and Changes in Consciousness**
  - Physical symptoms manifest without medical explanations. Alterations in one's state of mind can develop which include amnesia, heightened alertness, or dissociative symptoms.

Salter and Hall have discussed that CPTSD is an advanced form of PTSD. It is often found in people who have extensive childhood trauma

---

[57] Herman, J. L. (1992). Complex PTSD: A syndrome in survivors of prolonged and repeated trauma. *Journal of Traumatic Stress, 5*(3), 377-391.

and chronic experiences of interpersonal abuse.[58] CPTSD symptoms closely resemble dissociative identity disorder or borderline personality disorder. This can be confusing for therapists and clients alike because the treatment for each of these disorders can bring about different sets of challenges.

Working with complex trauma survivors is not for the faint of heart. The memories that replay in their minds are severe, persistent, and indescribable. Complex trauma can be caused by experiences we have as adults, such as exposure to violence or war, but it can also start in our childhood. Some people go through severe neglect, abuse, and events worse than most people can imagine. Childhood adversity has consistently been shown to be a major contributor to physical health issues in adulthood, including cancer, diabetes, stroke, and suicidality.[59]

A key aspect of complex PTSD is its interpersonal dimension. As I mentioned earlier, sufferers of CPTSD struggle with their internal experiences, but what's arguably the worst is the effect on their relationships. Violence is disorienting, especially when it involves those we trust. We end up experiencing it as a deep-rooted sense of betrayal. For this reason, we must discuss Dr. Jennifer Gómez's cultural betrayal trauma theory and Dr. Jennifer Freyd's concept of institutional betrayal.

Cultural Betrayal Trauma Theory

A study of the experiences of Black students at a predominantly white university found that violence and victimization are actually pretty common. They also found that ethno-cultural betrayal predicted post-traumatic stress symptoms. Ethno-cultural betrayal trauma occurs when

---

[58] Salter, M., & Hall, H. (2021). Reducing shame, promoting dignity: A model for the primary prevention of complex post-traumatic stress disorder. *Trauma, Violence, & Abuse, 23*(3), 906–919.

[59] van der Kolk, B. (2015). *The body keeps the score: Mind, brain and body in the transformation of trauma*. New York, NY: Penguin Random House.

someone of your own ethnicity, race, or culture harms you. According to cultural betrayal trauma theory, violence within racially diverse communities violates the solidarity, or (intra)cultural trust, that members of the community have to protect against outside racism. This makes cultural betrayal even more harmful than if someone of a different race or culture did it to you.

This could be due to the (intra)cultural pressure to not disclose that someone from your own culture has harmed you. We naturally seek to protect our own, so when someone from our "group" causes us harm, there's a higher chance the victim will get dissociative or complex trauma symptoms.[60]

We have psychological defenses against people who are different from us, but we get blindsided when the violence comes from within our own close-knit communities. For example, while there may be defenses against violence stemming from whiteness, these defenses are severely challenged when Black students are sexually assaulted by other Black students. This breach of (intra)cultural trust hurts Black people even more than violence from a white person because it bypasses the natural defenses we have against outsiders. Also, if there's pressure within your own culture not to tell anyone because it could be seen as betraying or snitching, the trauma becomes even harder to handle.

Once again, our identity plays a role in how we experience trauma. Gómez explains,[61] according to cultural betrayal trauma theory, cultural betrayal trauma predicts mental, behavioral, and physical health problems such as dissociation, suicide ideation, and cardiovascular issues. It also can impact how you see your own culture, leading to more internalized prejudice, stronger pressure from within your group, more

---

[60] Gómez, J. M. (2017). *Cultural betrayal trauma theory* [unpublished doctoral dissertation]. University of Oregon.

[61] Gómez, J. M. (2023). *The cultural betrayal of Black women and girls: A Black feminist approach to healing from sexual abuse* (pp. xvii-236). American Psychological Association.

distrust in your cultural group, and changes in how you view your own racial identity.[62]

Institutional Betrayal

About 35.6% of women worldwide have experienced sexual violence.[63] The prevalence of sexual violence is higher for women than men. It's mediated by cultural factors and is often linked to unequal power dynamics between the sexes.[64] This doesn't mean that men and boys don't experience sexual violence. It's just that we typically do not ask men about sexual violence, and sometimes they go their whole lives without telling anyone at all that it happened.[65] Gendered violence in close-knit communities is even worse when the community fails to take steps to protect its members or punishes individuals for their disclosures.

Betrayal causes post-traumatic stress symptoms because it involves attachment relationships that have evolved as basic survival mechanisms.[66] What's interesting is that these relationships do not have to be between people; they can also be between you and your workplace, your religious organization, or with entire institutions. Institutions create trusting relationships with their members and violations can also feel like deep-seated betrayals.

---

[62] Gómez, *The cultural betrayal of Black women and girls: A Black feminist approach to healing from sexual abuse* (pp. xvii-236). American Psychological Association.

[63] García-Moreno, C., Pallitto, C., Devries, K., Stöckl, H., Watts, C., & Abrahams, N. (2013). Global and regional estimates of violence against women: Prevalence and health effects of intimate partner violence and non-partner sexual violence. World Health Organization.

[64] Borumandnia, N., Khadembashi, N., Tabatabaei, M., & Alavi Majd, H. (2020). The prevalence rate of sexual violence worldwide: A trend analysis. *BMC Public Health, 20,* 1-7.

[65] United Nations High Commissioner for Refugees. (2012). Working with men and boy survivors of sexual and gender-based violence in forced displacement.

[66] Smith, C. P., & Freyd, J. J. (2013). Dangerous safe havens: Institutional betrayal exacerbates sexual trauma. *Journal of Traumatic Stress, 26*(1), 119–124.

For example, Smith and Freyd[67] found that when women in the military made complaints after experiencing sexual violence but still remained in the armed forces, they had increased difficulty coping. Powerful institutions often seek to maintain power and hierarchy, so they do not take very well to anything that can destabilize them. Not every organization has institutional courage, and when this is lacking, they may actively discourage disclosures, protect offenders, or even punish the victims. For these reasons, sexual assault survivors who felt betrayed by their institutions also reported higher levels of anxiety, sexual dysfunction, and dissociation, among other mental health consequences.

Dissociation and Diverse Identities

Identity-based discrimination is associated with some of the most complex post-traumatic stress symptoms. McClendon and colleagues[68] revealed that for veterans who had experienced discriminatory stress in the previous six months, both gender and race played a role. Those who had the most severe PTSD symptoms were Black women. Gender and race compounded stress more than race or gender on their own, meaning the stress was higher for Black women than for white women or Black men.

In another study, Keating, Muller, and Wyers[69] analyzed the experiences of people who identified as LGBTQ+. They were especially interested in those who linked their trauma to identity-based discrimination. The study involved 157 participants who had experienced trauma as well as data on their experiences of discrimination

---

[67] Smith & Freyd, 2013, 119-124.

[68] McClendon, J., Kressin, N., Perkins, D., Copeland, L. A., Finley, E. P., & Vogt, D. (2021). The impact of discriminatory stress on changes in posttraumatic stress severity at the intersection of race/ethnicity and gender. *Journal of Trauma & Dissociation*, 22(2), 170–187.

[69] Keating, L., Muller, R. T., & Wyers, C. (2021). LGBTQ+ people's experiences of barriers and welcoming factors when accessing and attending intervention for psychological trauma. *Journal of LGBTQ Issues in Counseling, 15(1)*, 77–92.

and psychological functioning. Those whose trauma was linked to discrimination had higher levels of attachment anxiety, attachment avoidance, emotion dysregulation, PTSD, and dissociative symptoms compared to those who did not.

Specific types of discrimination like homophobia, biphobia, and transphobia were positively correlated with greater mental health challenges. For those who experienced transphobia, a higher level of transgender congruence—meaning a greater alignment between one's internal sense of gender identity and their external appearance—appeared to mitigate mental health challenges. This led to them having lower levels of emotional dysregulation, PTSD, and dissociative symptoms.

Not all oppressed people experience oppression in the same way. Many times, it can be based on your race, your gender, or your own identity, but mainly, it is down to how your society classifies you in the context you find yourself in.

With these betrayal-based, intimate, or interpersonal forms of trauma the word dissociation comes up often. One of the foremost experts on the topic, Dr. Jamie Marich,[70] defines dissociation as the act of separating from the present moment, especially when the present is dangerous. Our behaviors, actions, and states of mind are meant to help us to adapt and navigate the world. Dissociation, too, even though it can be experienced as unpleasant, inconvenient, or even unpredictable, is a shift in our consciousness that is intended to help us cope with severe difficulty.

When life gets too threatening, a person might, almost without warning, numb their body, disconnect from reality, and even switch to different states of consciousness. We all go through difficulties to some degree, but some people have so many painful triggers from their past

---

[70] Marich, J. (2023). *Dissociation made simple: A stigma-free guide to embracing your dissociative mind and navigating daily life.* North Atlantic Books.

that their symptoms interfere with earning a living, maintaining relationships, and even their desire to stay alive. Suffering from discrimination, betrayals, and the neglect of our institutions can leave very deep wounds that are hard to heal without help.

Dissociation and the Binary Complex Trauma Cycle

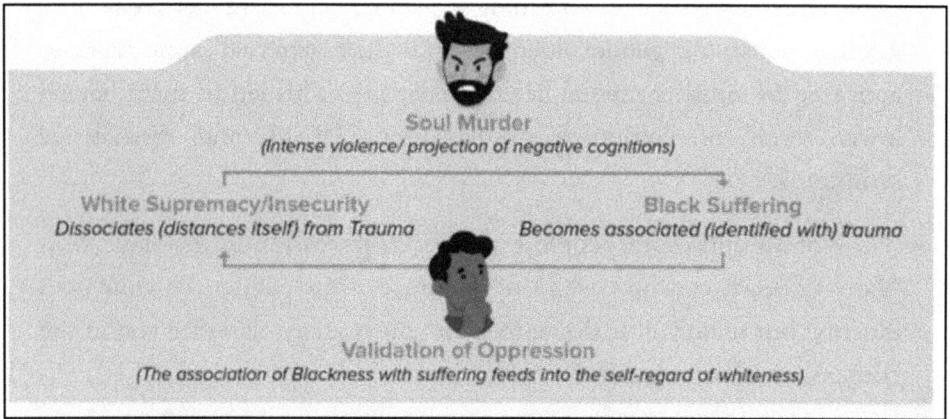

Image From: *Racial Trauma Recovery*

The binary complex trauma cycle shows how dissociation plays a role in maintaining violence in our social/political context. On the left, you will see what we call white supremacy/insecurity. This refers to the belief that some people are worth more than others and that it must be kept this way at all costs. In order to maintain this, whiteness must dissociate from any flaws or trauma that it has incurred in maintaining dominance.

The word "white" in some dictionaries is represented as devoid of blemishes, pure, or even holy. It is not a coincidence then that white supremacists will also see themselves in this way and, in some instances, align with religious ideology to reinforce their violent rhetoric. Even though violence may violate the tenets of these religions, that doesn't matter because it is not an issue of logic but of psycho-logic. As demonstrated in chapter two, none of this is supposed to be based on rationality, but power and fear.

The elements of white supremacy/insecurity are best represented by Dr. Frances Cress Welsing's definition. She describes white supremacy as being a local and global power system created by individuals classified as white. This system is made up of patterns of communication, emotional responses, specific actions, and several other domains. This takes place simultaneously in all areas of society, with the goal of preventing the genetic annihilation of those who are considered as white.

Welsing explains that non-white people are genetically dominant in terms of skin coloration, while white people's skin coloration is genetically recessive. Because the child of a darker- and lighter-skinned couple can potentially look darker-skinned, there is a fear that race mixing may eventually "exterminate" lighter-skinned people. This preoccupation with being replaced or becoming irrelevant creates an insecurity in the white consciousness, motivating the drive for self-preservation and the relentless pursuit of power.

This definition lets us know that white supremacy is based on fear. Naturally, then, it is only fair to pair white supremacy with insecurity. There have been a number of high-profile racist mass shootings in recent years, whether targeting African Americans in Florida, Asian Americans in Texas, or Muslim Canadians in Quebec City. The most despicable thing is that there are too many to list here.

Still, those who commit race-based mass violence rarely come from a place of superiority. Instead, their profiles consistently reveal backgrounds of inadequacy and resentment. Whether it involves the power structure or its followers, whenever extreme violence is an option, it is because extreme fear, insecurity, and impotence is their reality.

Soul Murder and Black Suffering

One main way that whiteness maintains such a powerful posture is through the process of soul murder. Shengold[71] defines this as a deliberate attempt to destroy the identity of one who has been marginalized. The goal is to make the target completely dependent on the perpetrator and to force them to betray their own values or beliefs without the perpetrator needing to give more orders. The result pushes the victim into a cycle, causing them to self-perpetuate their own destruction. Tactics like these are common when dealing with cases involving narcissistic abusers. This reveals why they have such control over their victims before the victims even know what hit them.

The process of soul murder creates black suffering. Black suffering is the total sum of the many ways the social context views and contextualizes people who are non-white. If we consider the historical associations in the West between whiteness and faultlessness, then those who are white's opposite, classified as "black," must be delegitimized at all costs. Their suffering reinforces the dominance of whiteness. It *must* happen not just through physical acts of terrorism but through any conceivable form of psychological violence. Blackness becomes the place where all of the negative traits that don't fit with the "perfect" image of whiteness can be conveniently relocated.

In our society, Black men are seen as uncontrollably hypersexual despite a history of white enslavers sexually assaulting Black men and women. Black people are stereotyped as being lazy despite being forced to work themselves to death. Hypocrisy is just an afterthought; if whiteness doesn't exist, blackness must be created to allow whiteness to exist.

---

[71] Shengold, L. (1991). *Soul murder: The effects of childhood abuse and deprivation.* BoD–Books on Demand.

Let me repeat this so it is clearer: since whiteness is an artificial construct, it must create and recreate blackness in order to define itself. But that's not all. The only way to justify violence is to first dehumanize the victim; the violence comes afterward. Soul murder is not just physical violence; it is an attack at all levels that seeks to remove the identity and erase the core of its victim. And this attack happens from all directions and all levels of society.

Rejecting such an intense level of violence is not easy. The victim convinces themselves that they have no choice but to believe what their oppressor thinks about them. In this case, then, blackness becomes associated with trauma. When the victim believes what black suffering communicates, when they fully embrace social defeat and own their shame, this validates the oppression. Not only do they suffer; they also start to believe they deserve it.

This cycle of soul murder is both an individual and interpersonal issue that can even show up as horizontal (lateral) violence. When sufficiently traumatized, Black people can become their own worst enemies. When the oppressor retreats into the distance, the trauma survivor still swings at whatever is within arm's reach. It often leads to bullying or degrading others just to get ahead. It's actually genius. The oppressor doesn't need to be involved if the victim does the dirty work.

The internalization of anti-Blackness, self-hatred, or shame because of our own identity is hard to admit. Sometimes it's even harder to do it in therapy. This is why Rhythm and Processing, which does not rely on disclosures like talk-therapy, is ideal for treating the internalization of racial trauma. We can address the dissociative symptoms that come from the horizontal violence and betrayals created by these oppressive systems. We can heal from the negative beliefs that carry overwhelming feelings beyond words. The binary complex trauma cycle causes oppressed people to become associated with trauma, but there is a way to revolutionize our thinking about all of this.

The Validation of White Supremacy/Insecurity

As I mentioned earlier, Black suffering is constantly created and recreated, but this cycle does not start with the victim. Whiteness constantly rejects and dissociates from any and all of its negative aspects while instead directing them towards Blackness. Dissociation plays a key role here as well. Because discussing one's crimes can be uncomfortable or unflattering, those who have the most power will downplay or cover up the worst of their violations.

A general model for how this happens in institutions is what Drs. Sarah Harsey and Jennifer Freyd labeled as DARVO.[72] This stands for Deny, Attack, Reverse Victim, and Offender. Abusers typically use this strategy, and it is often effective against people who are not trained in its use. When accused of violence, the first step is to deny what has happened. The second is to attack the credibility of the accuser, while the third is to reverse the roles of victim and offender.

Watch the actions of the powerful men who were accused during the #metoo movement. You will often see them deny or downplay the accusations, respond with name-calling or by smearing the accusers, and painting themselves as the real victims. This strategy has been frequently used by a certain infamous president of the United States,[73] and he has millions of supporters who stick with him because of his skillful use of it. When the careers of powerful people are threatened, they use this strategy to avoid consequences—and the sad thing is, it works.

Let's take another look at the role of whiteness in racial trauma. Its denial of the reality of racial trauma, along with its fragility and avoidance strategies, mirrors the psychological process of dissociation. To maintain

---

[72] Harsey, S., & Freyd, J. J. (2020). Deny, attack, and reverse victim and offender (DARVO): What is the influence on perceived perpetrator and victim credibility? *Journal of Aggression, Maltreatment & Trauma, 29*(8), 897–916.

[73] Brenner, I. (2021). Disinformation, disease, and Donald Trump. *International Journal of Applied Psychoanalytic Studies, 18*(2), 232-241.

its existence, whiteness must dissociate from its own trauma to sustain its illusion of moral superiority. This reversing the victim and offender strategy (from DARVO) is used strategically and conveniently whenever necessary.

Using our society's institutions to downplay the extent of soul murder installs the idea that Blackness is to blame for the trauma that whiteness causes. When Blackness is understood in this way, these projections validate the oppression, locking the binary complex trauma cycle in place. We can only get out of this once we know the rules of the game.

Let's go over a real-world example of this dissociative process. A study by Bor and colleagues[74] explored the mental health spillover effects of news reports about police killings. The impact of police killings significantly alters the mental health of Black Americans. Their estimates showed that the mental health burden from this form of violence is almost as large as the mental health impact of diabetes annually.

What is especially interesting is that Black Americans reported worse mental health days due to the killings of Black or white unarmed victims. On the other hand, in the case of white respondents in their sample, they demonstrated no significant increase in poor mental health days after killings, regardless of the victim's race. None.

The authors suggest that police killings have a significant impact on Black Americans, in part because of the institutions that usually protect the officers from legal consequences, and that state-sanctioned violence has been used to target people of African descent for centuries.

This results in an implied lower value of life for Black people—not just from law enforcement and legal institutions, but from society in

---

[74] Bor, J., Venkataramani, A. S., Williams, D. R., & Tsai, A. C. (2018). Police killings and their spillover effects on the mental health of black Americans: A population-based, quasi-experimental study. *The Lancet, 392*(10144), 302-310.

general. The authors point to the impact of structural racism on mental health outcomes and that police killings of unarmed Black Americans are manifestations of this hostile social context.

Those who are non-Black, and especially those who identify as white, cannot feel the same way about anti-Black violence. We are encouraged to be numb to the suffering of others. There's a social context that permits and, to some degree, encourages a lack of emotional participation. If non-Black people were to be just as bothered by anti-Black racism and see that it's not just a Black people problem, we might actually solve racism.

If white women were to see that the binary complex trauma cycle can easily substitute male dominance for white supremacy / insecurity and female submission for black suffering, we might be able to build intercommunal solidarity.[*]

If we can realize that the methods of colonization the Indigenous people confronted in North America are connected to what Frantz Fanon was telling us about in Martinique and what Steve Biko spoke about in South Africa, we might actually walk ourselves right into changing the world as we see it.

---

[*] However, color-blind feminism will always fall victim to the dynamics of white supremacy/insecurity. Many times, when activists are united for a cause, internalized whiteness can drive a wedge into true solidarity, threatening such movements. Studies have explained how the racism of white activists can contribute to burnout in racial justice activists of color. This includes white activists who secretly hold racist views and consciously or inadvertently sabotage the work of fellow activists, avoid standing up and using their privilege to defend others, are excessively fragile due to whiteness, or exploit or take credit for others' work. See: Gorski, P. C., & Erakat, N. (2019). Racism, whiteness, and burnout in antiracism movements: How white racial justice activists elevate burnout in racial justice activists of color in the United States. *Ethnicities, 19*(5), 784–808.

Summary

The binary complex trauma cycle describes the function of subjugation, propping up whiteness to the detriment of Blackness. These binaries suggest that there are clear-cut categories on either end. The oppressor uses soul murder to engender a self-perpetuating cycle of self-hatred and horizontal violence in the community that absorbs these violent projections.

Once the victim subscribes to this, it validates the violence and leads to more of it. Whiteness dissociates from trauma, while Blackness becomes associated with it. We are forced to identify with these illusory categories as a distraction. These distractions feed into race-based stereotypes and internalized oppression—images reinforced by the media, society, and multiple layers of communication. This prevents any form of solidarity from enshrining itself. Awaken to this.

There are no binaries that serve us. Humans do not fit into neatly packaged categories. Dispel the myth caused by the binary complex trauma cycle. Challenge the cycle, heal from the need to dissociate from suffering. Confront it and change the world.

In the next chapter, we will explore ways to adopt an empowering perspective—not one rooted in a deficit model but based on Africentric principles. We will also take a good look at how therapeutic change occurs by examining the process of memory reconsolidation.

CHAPTER 5

PRINCIPLES FOR CLINICAL PROGRESS

Turning the Tables on a Memory

Vijay, a young high school teacher with a quiet demeanor, was seeking a way of improving his self-esteem. He explained that though both of his parents were Indian, one of them was Scheduled Caste. His anxiety kept getting worse. He faced betrayals by his family members, rejection from the local community, and daily microaggressions because of his darker skin.

He had tried other therapies and was looking for something different. That's where we crossed paths. Our sessions gave him a space where he could turn the tables on the trauma he had inherited from the family, cultural, and political spheres of his life.

Sharing the screen of my computer, we scrolled through a list of previously established trauma targets.

"Ready to work on this colonization target?" I asked, acknowledging the courage it took for him to meet with me.

"Sure am," Vijay responded. His voice was a little shaky, but it held a glimmer of resolve.

We built trust over the course of our sessions. I was curious without prying, inquisitive without judgment. This gave us several sessions that disconfirmed his expectations about therapy. After teaching him self-care skills, learning a bit more about his family tree, and listing events that shook his self-esteem, we were now ready to begin the trauma reprocessing. This next question would allow us to set up the means of changing how his memory was stored forever.

"What's the most awesome video we can find online?"

"Oh? For real?" Vijay's eyes widened in surprise, his expression lit up, and he laughed. He never thought that he would be able to choose what the therapist would watch. He hesitated at first, choosing a video that did not necessarily make him feel good but would be socially accepted.

"Umm, I don't know, maybe this image of a cabin isn't doing it for me."

"Look," I said, "when I said awesome, I meant it. Let's choose something that you can't help but smile about."

We scrolled through a series of videos until a smile came to his face.

"I know! Let's choose this one."

"Oh, wow!"

Despite my practice with meditation and mindfulness, I had difficulty keeping back my smile, then my chuckle, and finally my laughter. A video of tiny poodles wearing even tinier top hats jumped onto the screen. Maybe it was the randomness of his choice or the never-ending question of why pet owners upload videos like this, but it really cracked me up.

Using the Rhythm and Processing technique and having disconfirming experiences put his concerns to rest. A smile stretched across his face and his worries melted away. Laughing and having fun was not against the rules of this therapy; in fact, they facilitated his recovery.

But what do dancing puppies have to do with trauma therapy? This chapter hopes to explain what underlies transformative change.

What Do We Need for Anti-Racist Therapy?

While developing the principles of anti-racist psychotherapy, I realized two things. First, many therapists do not come from an anti-racist perspective. This is a consequence of their training. Most popular forms of treatment offer little to nothing relating to race, ethnicity, or culture. This might have changed a little since the BLM protests of 2020, but only just enough to keep up "progressive" facades and any approach's share of the market. The result? Most therapists still maintain the illusion of a "neutral" or "color-blind" perspective, which is useless for confronting issues of racism. When our response to suffering is avoidance or fragility, which maintain the binary complex trauma cycle, then we reinforce the client's suffering.

Second, many therapists do not know precisely what causes therapeutic change. We have theories of change; we have hypotheses for change; we even have people who pride themselves on fancy terms and explanations to justify intractable pain in the lives of our clients. But that is not enough. Case conceptualization is important, but the resolution of suffering does not come from what the therapist knows, where the therapist studied, or which legacy admission university popped them out as an expert.

We need a clear understanding of the social/political factors that contribute to mental health challenges and an understanding of the mechanisms that lead to trauma recovery for all of us. Without that, we will end up creating a field that pathologizes the help-seekers, deepens the mentality of victim-blaming, or, even worse, perpetuates the falsehoods of biological determinism. When we understand what causes suffering and learn how to alleviate it, the therapist can step away from a prideful posture and adopt a framework that is more humane, more real, and ultimately more effective.

Anti-racist psychotherapy needs a different set of principles that take the hierarchies in our profession and flip them onto their heads. We need a defined mechanism based not on content but on the process of change, allowing for the greatest number of people to benefit. Therefore, this chapter will consider two helpful sets of ideas: Africentric principles and memory reconsolidation.

Africentric Principles

The Africentric principles that I base my practice on are best explained by Faye Belgrave and Kevin Allison. [75] They list seven dimensions that resonate well with African American clients and counter an exclusively Eurocentric worldview:

- Spirituality
- Collectivism
- Time
- Orality
- Affect and Emotion
- Balance and Harmony
- Verve and Rhythm

These concepts are essential for working with people of African descent and are also effective with individuals from various collectivist cultural backgrounds. In my practice, they have also been helpful in creating therapeutic change for people of all racial, gender, cultural, and social identities.

The Principles in a Therapeutic Context

Having long reflected on these principles and experimented with them in my practice, I have come to a number of conclusions about their role in racial trauma treatment. Let's discuss what they are and how each contributes to anti-racist psychotherapy.

---

[75] Belgrave, F. Z., & Allison, K. W. (2018). *African American psychology: From Africa to America.* Sage Publications.

Spirituality

Our lives carry a purpose. Spirituality as an Africentric principle keeps its usual sense of belief in a higher power or in a set of transcendent values. But in my understanding, it also includes the divinity within each individual, which blesses us all with an infinite creative potential, both within ourselves and beyond ourselves.

There is a deep meaning to our suffering, which can be transmuted into wisdom. We may not understand it based on our current circumstances, but it becomes clearer as we grow, heal, and recover. Even if we don't completely understand the current chapter of our lives, there is a higher purpose in the end. There is a "faith" that shapes our life's history, outside of any one specific religious belief. As people recover, they feel more connected to wonderful synchronicities.

Collectivism

The importance of reciprocity is undeniable. We are all one people, and we have to learn to work together and help each other. We are more than just individuals and more than the shallow "identities" that the social structure dictates for us. But it goes even deeper than that. We are all composed of different elements, and sometimes, when necessary, we can mobilize these different aspects of ourselves to help us.

There are parts of us that remain youthful, no matter our age. There are parts of us that hold wisdom, regardless of our experience. Some may be closely aligned with anger, sadness, joy, or fear. However, all members of our internal family system are precious and deserve healing. On our path of recovery, we strive not only to improve external relationships but, perhaps more importantly, to create peace among these internal aspects of ourselves.

As mentioned in the previous chapter, dissociation comes about due to a fracturing of our personality structure induced by trauma. Some parts of our personality can feel rejected or even grow to be at odds with other aspects of ourselves. This can lead them to take on different roles which include desperately preventing the most vulnerable parts from reaching consciousness or structuring one's life around avoiding future traumatization.[76] As we validate the needs of our internal family, we become more stable. We work toward harmony on the inside to live harmoniously on the outside.

Time

Time is flexible and malleable. When people heal from trauma, they often change how they see the past and alter the possibilities of the future.

The present is shaped by the past, meaning they are connected, and sometimes there is a rhythm that causes events to echo through time. People, along with their beliefs and traumas, always exist in relationship to the things that preceded them. We often mimic the parenting styles of our parents or gravitate toward partners whose attachment styles feel familiar. In this way, our present day relationships can usually be explained or justified by looking back into history.

Black people are made into figments of other people's imagination in a social structure that is frightened of its own traumatic past. This process limits the Black person to the white idea of them. As a result, Black people are conditioned to start their story with slavery, and white people are conditioned to see all of their progress as upward mobility, disconnecting them from their past history. This conveniently reinforces and validates the binary complex trauma cycle, reinforcing a starting point that centers the past around suffering while denying people of African descent access to their true history.

Dr. Greg Carr, a master scholar and professor of Africana studies at Howard University, often phrases this as the loss of the "momentum of memory." Our being denied access to our history, best represented by

---

[76] Schwartz, R. C., & Sweezy, M. (2019). *Internal family systems therapy*. Guilford Publications.

the recent banning of books at the behest of conservative politicians and white nationalist interest groups, revises history in order to control the future of our education.

In a therapeutic context, we are easily sidetracked by time. We can get lost in our misunderstanding of the client's history due to our own miseducation. A recent history of slavery does not determine who a person is today or who they were before that. Knowing that Black culture existed before slavery opens up the idea of what Black culture was and can be. Knowing that trauma survivors existed before their trauma helps us envision a future without it.

Orality

We must reclaim our narrative. There is so much said about Black people, even though we are conditioned to see ourselves as "marginalized." Our music is ubiquitous; our actors, mannerisms, and speech are popular. But whose Black are we being when we call ourselves Black? There is great power in reclaiming one's own narrative or choosing how to identify rather than accepting someone else's. The negative beliefs many of us hold came from someone else. What happens when we change our narrative?

. OOur words carry a weight. The negative beliefs we've learned from our trauma history affect how we feel. Saying "I'm not good enough" never feels better than saying "I can do it." Imagine truly believing one or the other in the core of your spirit. Naturally, this would also change the feeling. The words resonate within us differently. When we change our feelings through our words, we also change the actions that are available to us. Repeating this process can permanently alter our beliefs about who we are and who we are meant to become.

An important part of anti-racist psychotherapy involves having clients choose words in their own language that they associate with positive states of mind. As I write this in English, I am using a colonizer's language, an imperfect medium that can never fully convey the full range of emotions, dreams, and ambitions of my clients from all corners of the world.

For this reason, I ask them to use words that are closest to their heart when they think of inspiring visualizations and especially affirmations. Just this past month, I heard Québécois French, African American Vernacular English, Kanien'kéha (Mohawk), and Lebanese Arabic in my sessions. When we give ourselves permission to think and speak in our mother tongue, the words just hit different.

Affect and Emotion

We live by integrity, not by our trauma history. It is not just the words we carry in our minds. Our bodies also carry wisdom. How we feel is deeply related to what we believe about ourselves, our relationships, and even our environment. As I said earlier when we spoke about trauma, the nervous system reacts in a survival-based manner when threatened. Stress from the environment is communicated by the body.

We feel it from our accelerated heart beats, tightness in the stomach, and sometimes the feelings can even be dissociated from the physical body. The mind has interesting and innumerable methods of communicating the full range of the human experience. Trauma survivors become so inundated with these stressful messages that it becomes difficult to trust their "gut feeling" and easier to confuse it with the residue of painful memories.

It is a spectrum. Severely traumatized people often report feeling disconnected from or numb to their bodies. But as we heal from our suffering, people often describe a lighter or clearer feeling throughout their bodies. Their purpose, motivations, and self-determination increase as they learn to make decisions based on their integrity instead of their trauma history.

Balance and Harmony

We are drawn to moments of mindfulness. As we work through our past, there arises a greater awareness of the present moment. It is important to bring in the Kemetic principle of Ma'at. This is a concept too deep to explain here, but in simple terms it refers to balance, order, harmony, justice, and truth.

As we uphold our principles, we experience greater peace. As people gain greater self-awareness, they redefine their values as well as who they should be spending their time with. We learn to distinguish between selfishness, selflessness, and self-love. Boundaries for time and energy become clearer, and reciprocal relationships become sought after. The person breaks the old pattern of reactivity and auto-pilot functioning and seeks experiences that reaffirm and re-establish balance.

Verve and Rhythm

There is an energy and uniqueness in all people. There are ups and downs, ebbs and flows, but with time, we realize there is more than one way to live our lives, more than one way to be. We can choose a different path and still be authentic. There are many ways to be, do, and exist in the world.

Ask yourself these questions:

- Who am I without my suffering?
- Who will I become once I choose to be a cycle breaker?
- What makes me feel enthusiastic?
- What self-care plans do I need to cultivate to achieve balance?
- Instead of playing the same old song, what will my identity look like once I pull it up, take it from the top and remix it to my own liking?

Answering these questions adds a greater depth to our humanity. Traumatization limits our experiences. Recovery allows us to love who we want, be who we want, and live however we want rather than conforming to the will of others. We heal when we can rediscover and recreate our unique way of being in the world. There is more than one way to be Black, more than one way to be a human, more than one way to exist in this world.

By cultivating an awareness of the Africentric principles, we can resolve problems relating to social identity stressors, complex trauma, and race-based stresses. If mental illness is a limiting label that constricts, mental health is an open-ended category that expands.

When we as therapists acknowledge these principles in trauma recovery, refrain from imposing our agenda, and work on the internalization of identity-based oppression that exists in *all* of us, then we can have honest discussions. Let's not recoil in shock when a Black person who doesn't fit our preconceived notions shows up in the therapy room. Let's humanize our psychotherapy. In chapter six, I will explain more explicitly how Rhythm and Processing incorporates these principles.

The Process of Memory Reconsolidation

Let's take a look back to our neurobiological perspective. To understand complex trauma, we need to understand how memories impact us and how we can change our recollection of them. Memory reconsolidation is an important neurological process. It happens whenever someone recalls previously stored memories, then re-stores them with updated information.

This is helpful with traumatic memories, which are often filled with highly emotional content. When we are able to update or modify how a given memory is stored, this allows us to change how we relate to it. To do this, we must "annul" or cancel the previous associations that the traumatic material created in our minds. Ecker and Vaz explain the process.[77]

Generally, the process of unlearning through memory reconsolidation involves three subprocesses:

- **Recall:** re-experience the targeted emotional learning.
- **Destabilization:** produce a contradictory experience, a prediction error that destabilizes the targeted learning.
- **Re-encoding:** repeat the pairing of the two experiences. This counter-learning allows the nullification of the destabilized target learning.

Let's dive into some concrete examples. In the passages that follow, the therapist will have instructed the client to choose a target to work on and to also select an online video to be played for the purpose of destabilizing the target material. The therapist will then press play on the video and provide additional instructions while the video is playing. This will activate the memory mismatch that's required for the memory reconsolidation sequence.

It's never fun to think about stressful memories. But because we are using an unconventional approach, the client will feel differently from what they would typically predict. Repeating this process will destabilize the target memory and allow it to be re-encoded.

Working with Phobias

- **Issue:** The client has a phobia of his boyfriend's cat but wants to move in with him.
- **Recall:** During a session, he is instructed temporarily to imagine the experience of being around this cat.

---

[77] Ecker, B., & Vaz, A. (2022). Memory reconsolidation and the crisis of mechanism in psychotherapy. *New Ideas in Psychology, 66,* 100945.

- **Destabilization:** A set of disconfirming experiences occur; the client moves the memory out of his consciousness, and the therapist plays a video on the computer screen. It is a short snippet of the client's favorite comedy special. The client smiles with delight.
- The therapist provides instructions to help him focus. As the client chuckles while focusing on the show, a discrepancy is created between what he initially expected from focusing on the issue and what he actually feels in the present.
- **Re-encoding:** Through repeated exposure to feelings of joy and calm, alternating between checking with the memory and feeling the disconfirming experience, the original, fearful memory is updated. This leads the client to experience less fear about the cat and to form a different association to being in the same room as the animal.
- Even after one session, this can significantly reduce the phobic response. In my clinical experience, recovery from phobic responses can take one to three processing sessions. But everyone is different, so sometimes it could take more in order to be fully addressed.

Memory of Psychiatric Episode

- **Issue:** The client was recently overwhelmed due to a racial microaggression that related to their mental health.
- **Recall:** The client thinks about a time they were hospitalized due to a psychiatric episode, which was at the core of their intrusive thoughts during the moment of the microaggression.
- **Destabilization:** A set of disconfirming experiences occur. The image is contained and moved out of consciousness. The therapist plays a video of a Japanese onsen (public bath) on a computer screen.

- The therapist provides instructions to help the client focus. The client feels at peace while watching the steam rise from the pool, perhaps remembering what it felt like the last time they went on vacation. This creates a discrepancy between what they expected and what they actually experience in the present.

- **Re-encoding:** After multiple, repeated exposures and experiences of relaxation, the vividness of the memory associated with hospitalization decreases, the frustration from the microaggression diminishes, and the event triggering the crisis can no longer be recalled with any emotional reactivity.

- Memories of hospitalizations can be stressful for people who have experienced psychiatric episodes. Reconsolidating this memory on its own will not remove the entire diagnosis, but it definitely helps in reducing triggers that can provoke future episodes.

The mind makes associations between events, people, and our beliefs. These associations can sometimes be varied and unpredictable. This is why we need to use our creativity to target these associations with disconfirmation that can be visual (remembered experiences), auditory (music from streaming websites), or even somatic (feelings of awesomeness).

The events in the life of a complex trauma survivor may include betrayal trauma, as explained in chapter four, but can manifest in various forms such as phobias, recurring nightmares, suicidal ideation, addictions, encounters with law enforcement, or body dysmorphic associations. The upside is that we now have reliable methods to help people heal from these and other problematic memory associations.

Transformational Change through Experiences

Change is experiential. This is what underlies many of the successful attempts to help people who suffer from deep-rooted trauma. People heal through experiences, and these experiences change how we remember previous events. It is more than just the words of the therapist or the sound of a friend's voice consoling you during dark times. It is about what you experienced in your mind and body because of their communication.

Let me break it down. We have two general forms of memory, as Levine[78] explains: explicit and implicit. Explicit memories are more like data—where you were raised, your name, what happened on a specific date, etc. Implicit memory, on the other hand, stores emotional and procedural memories. This includes information based on survival, automatic impulses, instinctual urges, and even physical sensations that can leave us speechless.

The heart of trauma resides in implicit memory, and it is here that healing can take place by using memory reconsolidation. Ecker and Vaz[79] believe that therapists need to know why and how change occurs. They explain that stable, transformational change occurs through memory reconsolidation when the following three things take place:

- One or more symptoms of a problem completely disappear.
- The emotional activation related to the symptom disappears and doesn't come back.
- Both of the above occur and persist without any preventive measures.

---

[78] Levine, P. A. (2015). *Trauma and memory: Brain and body in a search for the living past: A practical guide for understanding and working with traumatic memory.* North Atlantic Books.

[79] Ecker & Vaz, Memory reconsolidation and the crisis of mechanism in psychotherapy.

Now tell me, why would anyone *not* want to use this kind of approach? Memory reconsolidation is the brain's way of changing what you experience in the present by updating what is stored in your memory of the past.

How Do We Do This?

The memory reconsolidation process occurs when we change how a memory is stored. Instead of staying in a stable or consolidated state, it needs to move to a destabilized or labile state in which it can be re-encoded differently. Again, this requires two things:

1. Reactivating the target memory.
2. Creating a discrepancy so that something different happens than what the memory would suggest.

Let's review it once more so we're clear.

- If the trauma involved being hospitalized after a dog bite, you might associate all dogs with being in a survival state.
- The prediction error occurs when you see an image of a dog, but instead of feeling fear, you feel awesome, neutral, or at peace.
- This causes a memory mismatch, where your current experience ends up being very different from the many previous times the memory was triggered, recalled, or thought about.

In terms of the prediction error, Ecker[80] explains that what's most important is not the specific procedure but what the person experiences because of it. It's not about the content; it's about the process.

---

[80] Ecker, B. (2018). Clinical translation of memory reconsolidation research: Therapeutic methodology for transformational change by erasing implicit emotional learnings driving symptom production. *International Journal of Neuropsychotherapy*, 6(1), 1–92.

Basically, if we can trigger a mismatch after recalling a memory, there is a window of time in which we can create a transformative change. This is helpful because if we are dealing with racial trauma or complex trauma, we cannot settle for ineffective solutions or those that just reinforce the learning from suffering.

Putting It All Together

I agree with Ecker about this process and even about how to do it.[*] But where we differ is in how to use this in a therapeutic context. What we present during that labile period does not need to be directly linked with the memory's underlying message. I believe Ecker uses memory reconsolidation this way because he is seeking to alter a person's cognitive schema; this is why his approach requires the disconfirmation to be very specific.

What we are doing in this form of therapy is to use disconfirming experiences to reprocess traumatic memories. For this reason, the Focus/COM Video works very well, even if it is not as specific as his methods. We are not attempting to change the whole neighborhood but to target the address where the traumatic memory lives.

Because we covered implicit memory, we already know that while some memories have overt messages behind them, not all of them do. Some clients with complex PTSD have symptoms that look like severe forms of dissociation, kicking them out of their bodies or preventing them using any words to describe what is going on.

We need to get back to the basics. We need to change how the person feels about their problem in order to solve it. Words are not enough. The body doesn't speak English, Mandarin, or Swahili. So, the

---

[*] I previously discussed this in *Racial Trauma Recovery*, where I explain Ecker's therapeutic reconsolidation process and discuss additional studies that support memory reconsolidation.

solution needs to be in a universal language that the body understands. What better way than to feel calm, motivated, or completely awesome?

We are using a *somatic-based* form of memory reconsolidation, leveraging the technological advances in our field. The method is based on the fundamental concept of memory reconsolidation and building on Ecker's theories. However, our focus is on targeting the specific memories that house the negative beliefs that connect to the deep-seated implicit memory material at the core of the trauma.

This is the foundation of the Rhythm and Processing strategies. We need to turn the tables on our suffering. To do this, we must maximize the use of prediction errors to challenge the patterns that the brain has been conditioned to repeat. We need to ensure that those we call clients can become the best therapists they have ever met. This approach represents a revolution in how we think about therapy and the healing that can result from it.

Summary

This chapter concerns the synergy between Africentric principles and memory reconsolidation. Thinking of Vijay at the beginning of the chapter, we can adopt approaches that are culturally respectful while using cutting-edge technology. We have the potential for a transformative framework based on anti-racist psychotherapy.

Our lives are purposeful. We are members of a global community, and cultivating our unique voices matter. By understanding the brain's intrinsic ability to heal and recover, we can promote healing by bringing in the client's interests, culture, and identity.

This is an invitation for therapists and clients alike to experience a therapy that turns the tables on the trauma. In the next chapter, we will dive deeper into the Rhythm and Processing strategies to learn more about what they look like in action.

CHAPTER 6

NOVEL INTERVENTIONS AND NEW DIMENSIONS

Changing How We See the Past

Nina, a Cree woman from Northern Quebec, sat across from me in the virtual therapy environment. Her presence, even though slightly digitized by her internet connection, still carried the strength of her Indigenous ancestors.

We sat in silence as she rhythmically tapped on her shoulders from left to right. I followed with my own bilateral tapping as well. The target had to do with pre-birth trauma, and that was all I knew. The content of the memory and my clinical interpretation of it was nowhere near as important as disconfirming her experience right here and right now.

"Take in a deep breath," I said, "and let it go."

We both exhaled. A feeling of calmness entered the session. Even though we were working virtually, the result was the same. She was able to completely reduce her stress to zero through a combination of exposure to a video of her favorite hip-hop song and tapping from shoulder to shoulder.

"And when you think about the trauma target now, what happens?"

Nina closed her eyes and appeared to scan through her body, rolling her shoulders, gently stretching her back.

"Wow." She breathed a sigh of relief. "It's all gone. I can barely see the memory anymore."

Nina smiled in astonishment. She gained a renewed sense of her cultural pride. Her friends noticed, her family noticed, and the feelings of imposter syndrome at the workplace faded into her long-term memory. It sure must look like magic to those who don't understand it, but miracles become a daily event when we use the right technology.

When working through trauma, we must be prepared and use the right tools. This chapter outlines my approach called Rhythm and Processing Strategies. It was created to eliminate the mental health consequences of racial trauma. Traditional approaches rarely take into account race or complex trauma. But this is different. The evolution of EMDR therapy and the subsequent development of Rhythm and Processing Strategies demonstrate the need for culturally responsive and complex-trauma-focused interventions.

EMDR Therapy: Shapiro's Discovery

Dr. Francine Shapiro developed EMDR therapy after first observing the usefulness of bilateral eye movements.[81] The model she crafted in the late 1980s emerged from her journey to heal from her own suffering. After being diagnosed with cancer, she researched and studied approaches that could solve problems of the mind and body.

As the story goes, Shapiro saw a connection between her thoughts, the movement of her eyes, and the result of feeling much calmer in mind and body. When she alternated between moving her eyes from left to right, she started to see that she was able to reduce the negative charge of the thoughts in her mind. Testing this technique with others, she eventually developed it into a structured method that has helped many thousands of people heal from stressful memories.

Since then, EMDR therapy has developed into an evidence-based approach with high-quality studies to back up its effectiveness. The Department of Veterans Affairs, the Department of Defense, and even the World Health Organization recognize it as a first-line treatment for post-traumatic stress disorder.[82]

---

[81] Shapiro, F. (2018). *Eye movement desensitization and reprocessing (EMDR) therapy (3rd ed.): Basic principles, protocols, and procedures.* Guilford Press.

[82] Shapiro, *Eye movement desensitization and reprocessing (EMDR) therapy.*

The Adaptive Information Processing Model

Integral to EMDR therapy is an information-processing model called Adaptive Information Processing (AIP). On this, I will paraphrase Dr. Andrew Leeds,[83] a renowned EMDR therapy trainer, instructor, and pioneer in treating PTSD, depression, and dissociative disorders. As he explains, the AIP model consists of three principles.

The First AIP Principle

All people have the innate capability to recover from trauma.

Although the actual number of trauma survivors is probably higher than we think, not all of them would meet the criteria to be diagnosed with a disorder. Why? Because all people have the ability to recover naturally. Most people do not have PTSD or complex PTSD or even complex forms of racial trauma. Sure, we are wired for survival, but we are also wired for homeostasis, or balance. Some people recover without therapy or medication. It is only when things don't line up as they should that these traumatic memories become stuck or distorted in our minds. Taking all this into account, if we are in a context that promotes healing, we can and will heal.

The Second AIP Principle

Trauma is encoded in a maladaptive form in our memory system.

Still, even if we can naturally find ways to recover, some stressful events can overwhelm what your nervous system can tolerate. This happens either because of its intensity, its frequency, or even your vulnerability at the time the event happens. If we go through intense stresses when we are infants and no one is there to hold or soothe us,

---

[83] Leeds, A. M. (2016). *A guide to the standard EMDR therapy protocols for clinicians, supervisors, and consultants (2nd ed.)*. Springer Publishing Company.

the body remembers this. In a way, it becomes easier to feel abandoned because it already happened in the past.

Let me use some computer metaphors for a second. Some events become stored in a maladaptive file format. It is like these memories get saved to your hard drive and take up space in a way where you can't reach them without crashing your computer. Sometimes our dysfunctional memories can even act like a virus and infect other data. It can infect your beliefs about yourself, your relationships, and the other files in your brain's storage. This is why when you try to access the "infected" thoughts, you relive it instead of thinking about it from a distance.

This is often at the core of mental health issues: something happened, exceeds what we can handle, so we store it in our heads differently. The way how it is stored creates an association to the past that disturbs you in the present.

The Third AIP Principle

Dual attention to both the memory of the trauma and to bilateral stimulation reengages our adaptive information processing.

When we use the structured protocols of EMDR therapy, paired with bilateral movements, and focus our attention on the traumatic memory, we reengage our ability to adapt. Bilateral stimulation usually involves the eyes, but can also include shoulder tapping, foot tapping, or thigh patting. No matter the method, the pace of the movement is agreed upon by both the client and therapist.*

---

* Of course, it is still not as easy as I make it sound here. Tuning into a traumatic memory can sometimes be retraumatizing without adequate preparation or sufficient resources. For some people, just thinking about tuning into a trauma can be overwhelming and terrifying. It can also take several sessions before people see improvement, especially for complex trauma survivors. This is why EMDR therapy requires training and is done by skilled professionals who are certified to provide this type of treatment.

Why would eye movement cause any of this? Because eyesight is necessary for survival. Leeds explains that alternating eye movements are necessary for threat detection and investigation.[84] The client recalls the trauma and then notices they're in a place of safety, such as being with a caring therapist. Their eyes may scan the environment many, many times in a single session. Alternating and repeating this "orienting" response helps to restore homeostasis and balance to our nervous systems.[85]

This orienting response also seems to explain why, even without eye movements, bilateral tapping on one's shoulders gives a similar benefit. These are not the only explanations for why bilateral stimulation is effective. Other mechanisms of action have also been hypothesized, and I have listed them in my previous work.[86] Still, the three principles listed above help to explain what EMDR therapy is and why we use it.

But even though EMDR therapy is effective, some of my clients have struggled with the third principle of the AIP. As I have written about in *Racial Trauma Recovery*, some people find it difficult to process using the standard protocol of EMDR therapy. Some of my clients would get discouraged. Therapists have consulted with me saying the same thing. It led me to think differently, seeking training, learning multiple approaches, and studying with experts in mental health. All of this was done to find a way to help those who needed it, especially people suffering from complex trauma symptoms.

---

[84] Leeds, A. M. (2016). *A guide to the standard EMDR therapy protocols for clinicians, supervisors, and consultants.* Springer Publishing Company.

[85] Siegel, D. J. (2012). *The developing mind: How relationships and the brain interact to shape who we are.* 2nd edn. Guilford Press.

[86] Archer, D. (2021). *Anti-Racist psychotherapy: Confronting systemic racism and healing racial trauma.* Each One Teach One Publications.

Rhythm and Processing Strategies

Over the past few years, EMDR therapy has been growing in popularity. I've seen it used in television dramas, even if it was overly dramatized, and I've even seen it endorsed by Hollywood celebrities. I can't get mad at anyone learning about EMDR from a TV show. What's even more important is that people know there are options for healing.

When I was looking for options as an addictions counselor in an Indigenous community, I was grateful to be introduced to EMDR therapy. We needed it. A lot of people got better. The more that I developed my practice, using EMDR for years with diverse groups in Montreal led me to develop an approach that extended from it. This led to the emergence of something new.

At first, Rhythm and Processing (RAP) was only meant to support EMDR therapy. Under the guidance of mentors, consultants, and client feedback, we have transformed RAP into an approach that can be adapted to work with a variety of other approaches and it can even be used on its own in some cases. Most psychotherapies do not focus on the needs of complex trauma survivors, especially in the realm of racial trauma. RAP was made to help fill that gap.

It's an approach that breathes life into therapy. RAP came about from trying to fill in the blanks for the other therapeutic approaches and adding an element of humanity in there. I was looking for a way to understand the client's problem without victim blaming, to validate without reinforcing stuckness, and to solve problems, period. At its current level of development, it achieves what I intended, which was to eliminate the mental health consequences of racial trauma.

Once again, Rhythm and Processing is more than a technique: it is a strategic way of looking at therapy and guiding people toward recovery. Though it was originally designed for racial trauma, because of the binary complex trauma cycle, it ends up working for anyone caught up in the

the spectrum of diverse identities. How does it do this? Because it challenges the binary of the therapy context itself.

There are times where the therapist is silent and guided by the client. There are also times where the client determines the path and tools for change. There is a therapeutic dance between the two, neither leading without the other's support. The rhythm they follow creates a truly client-centered therapy. The goal is to achieve what the client has set out for each session.

The process of change is based on a neurobiological understanding of trauma recovery and memory reconsolidation, Africentric principles that structure the intention of our interventions, and the four cores of Anti-Racist Psychotherapy that simplify the process for case conceptualization. We want people to experience disconfirming events that challenge their limiting beliefs and radically change their perspective on the traumatic memories that have haunted them.

Sounds good, right? Then let's go over the main strategies that make up Rhythm and Processing.

Mindfulness-Based Strategies

We all have the capacity to feel grounded and connected to the present moment.[87] I have written about how the social structure can steal our focus and how we have a responsibility to reclaim our mindfulness through practice, diligence, and the cultivation of self-love. Although *Black Meditation* was focused on cultivating a positive racial identity and managing daily stresses, it turns out that these ideas also apply to the spectrum of trauma.

For trauma survivors, the experience of dissociation was originally used to cope with the past. It always starts as being adaptive. It knocks

---

[87] Archer, D. (2021). *Black meditation: Ten practices for self-care, mindfulness, and self-determination.* Each One Teach One Publications.

you out of the present moment when things get too tough. But when dissociation gets out of control, being in a near endless state of overwhelming feelings or being disconnected from the present can be really disorienting. When we are dealing with trauma, there are times when a person needs to get back into the present moment so they can prevent themselves from being drawn back into the abyss of their suffering.

The key to this is sensation. We need practices and techniques that can help us to use the mind to calm the body and use the body to calm the mind. To help support people who are stressed in the present moment, we can use the guided Earth meditation and the mindful color breathing technique.

The guided Earth meditation is intended to help one connect to their body and to the planet in a grounding, intentional way. Breathing at regular and comfortable rhythms, we can gain the benefit of stress relief. It guides clients to notice different body parts that we usually take for granted and also instructs them to visualize their connection to something much greater than themselves, and that's the planet.

The mindful color breathing technique is a remixed version of a standard meditation. It's more of an active application of mindfulness. Using our imagination and ability to visualize, we can calm the stresses of the body. The meditator brings their attention to stressful sensations and identifies the underlying emotion. Next, they imagine what the corresponding color would be, and finally they breathe in a different color that neutralizes the stress.

Both of these applied forms of mindfulness are used strategically. They help the therapist with their assessment and help the client to learn more about their body and mind. When used in session, the therapist learns:

- Is the client comfortable following my instructions?

- Can the client easily access states of calm?
- Are there any obstacles they have with visualizing?

The client also finds answers to their own questions as well:

- Am I able to feel good when I need to?
- Can I safely access parts of my body?
- Can I really reduce physical and emotional pains using my imagination?

There's another component to the meditations. This one involves writing. The five grateful things writing exercises are also integral to mindful explorations. The five grateful things exercise involves journal writing as well as consciously listing five experiences of gratitude. The result is that the client becomes comfortable with the somatic experience of gratitude and becomes comfortable naming "gratitude" as an emotional state they can access.

Gratitude can only be experienced in the present moment. It involves taking into account your present, past, and future and being thankful for something that you have or that has taken place. Cultivating this practice leads to normalizing it and increases your ease of recognizing it. When we practice recognizing how our nervous system represents gratitude—noting its physical location, sensation, and movement—this awareness becomes an anchor. It helps trauma survivors to defend against intrusive thoughts, feelings of hopelessness, and cope with lower-level dissociative symptoms.

Motivational Interviewing

Motivational interviewing was developed by Miller and Rollnick.[88] When I was working as an addictions counselor, I always kept a number of their interventions in my back pocket. It has been a lifesaver for people who suffer from substance abuse and addiction.

When we think about drugs and alcohol, their purpose is to change how you feel in the present. There is so much overlap between substance abuse and trauma. Just like the trauma survivor, addicts also have difficulty feeling comfort in the present moment. So it is sad to say, but it makes sense that the person who hurts from their past uses medicine to cope with their pain in the present. This is why targeting the traumatogenic events of the past is one of the best ways of supporting those gripped by the clutches of addiction.

But even before touching the trauma, people have to be ready, willing, and able to even receive treatment. There are specific strategies, which I outline in *Racial Trauma Recovery*, that follow the suggestions from MI designed to improve empathy for the client, support their ability to change, increase discrepancies to influence motivation, and navigate through resistance.

I have been greatly inspired by MI's perspectives, and there is an approach I have adapted for substance abusers and trauma survivors. This helps me to develop a treatment plan that comes from the client while addressing the ambivalence that naturally comes from going to see a therapist. The client provides the benefits and disadvantages of maintaining the status quo and also the pros and cons of healing from their suffering.

This challenges what clients expect from therapy. We often focus on the problems the client comes in with or the benefits they are seeking,

---

[88] Miller W. R., & Rollnick, S. (2002). *Motivational interviewing: Preparing people for change*. Guilford Press.

but we rarely discuss the advantages of their suffering or the downsides of recovering. We do this because meeting people where they are at validates the parts of them that are hesitant to change. This also clarifies their motivation for change.

There's an additional disconfirmation that happens. They put themselves in the driver's seat once they end up listing the advantages and disadvantages without being scolded or lectured about it by the therapist. We end up challenging the hierarchy. The client becomes the expert, listing the limiting beliefs that prevent them from achieving their goals and the values that will motivate them to complete the goals of their therapy.

Structural Dissociation

Trauma can damage a person's mind. When it is severe and happens at vulnerable times in a person's life, its effects can be devastating. Survivors of adversity can become overwhelmed by flashbacks; some become so disoriented they find it hard to deal with life in general. Dissociation, one of the many ways of coping with trauma, can lead us to become disconnected from the very communities that we once knew and loved.

Van der Hart, Nijenhuis, and Steele[89] explain that when trauma gets to the point where it leads to extreme threats to a person's sense of safety, there can be a structural dissociation of the personality that explains these complex and sometimes confusing symptoms. What makes this complicated is that only some therapists specialize in working with dissociation or complex trauma. It just so happens that the overlap between complex racial trauma and complex PTSD necessitates, at a bare minimum, some basic knowledge of how to work with both populations.

---

[89] van der Hart, O., Nijenhuis, E. R., & Steele, K. (2006). *The haunted self: Structural dissociation and the treatment of chronic traumatization.* Norton.

The symptoms of complex racial trauma survivors can involve a structural dissociation of the personality. Similar to complex PTSD, major or even everyday racial trauma events can set the stage for complex racial trauma. Cenat[90] argues that racial trauma is technically always "complex." This is because of its pervasiveness and its destructive effects on both the mental and physical health of its victims. But even with their similarities, he explains that complex racial trauma differs from complex trauma in three ways. I'll give some short examples to explain:

- **Its origins**
  - Complex racial trauma occurs because of a social/political context that maintains white supremacy/insecurity.
  - Complex trauma can involve oppression but is not always about social identity factors.
- **Its constancy beyond childhood**
  - The experience of racial microaggressions or extreme racial violence can increase or decrease because of one's family systems context, relationships, geographic location, or economic status.
  - Complex trauma, in comparison, is usually associated with early attachment wounds or key developmental periods.
- **Its internalization**
  - For complex racial trauma survivors, for example, the message of Black suffering leads to negative beliefs not only about oneself but also about anyone else with the same identity. They assume their oppressor's view on their whole cultural group.
  - Complex trauma survivors see themselves in a bad light, but they rarely project their negative beliefs onto other large groups of strangers. They also assume their oppressor's

---

[90] Cénat, J. M. (2023). Complex racial trauma: Evidence, theory, assessment, and treatment. *Perspectives on Psychological Science, 18*(3), 675–87.

view, but it is mostly limited to themselves, not their social identity.

Polyvagal Theory

Developed by Stephen Porges at the University of Illinois' Brain-Body Center in the 1990s, this theory helps us understand the stress responses that trauma survivors have because of their trauma. Other researchers have found ways of making it more applicable to mental health practitioners.[91]

The autonomic nervous system helps us to navigate our environment by three different pathways: the sympathetic branch, the dorsal vagus, and the ventral vagus. The latter two are initiated by the parasympathetic nervous system. The dorsal vagal uses *immobilization* to respond to threats to survival, the sympathetic branch uses *mobilization* to avoid temporary threats to safety, and the ventral vagal uses *social engagement* to seek safety.

The dorsal vagal branch is generally associated with a "freeze" response. This is especially present when a person feels "disconnected" from their body or in a state of hypoarousal. Think of this as a deer looking into a vehicle's oncoming headlights in the middle of the night. She becomes immobilized, temporarily disconnected from her body and also from the present moment.

The sympathetic nervous system refers to the fight-or-flight survival response. This is when people are in a state of over-activation or hyperarousal. Think of a schoolyard bully's fists shaking with rage while trying to intimidate someone. Or another example, the same insecure bully running for his life after hearing he's going to be called to the principal's office. Fight or flight reactions happen when we're

---

[91] Dana, D. (2018). *The Polyvagal theory in therapy: Engaging the rhythm of regulation.* Norton.

responding to something we feared in the past or something to be feared in the future.

The ventral vagal response is when a person feels connected to the present, socially engaged, and secure in themselves. Think of the last time something or someone made you feel at peace, comfortable, and in a state of gratitude. Maybe there was a light feeling in the body. Maybe there was a smile on your face. Even if it's a glimmer from the past, remember the good feeling and you'll feel it.

When we help people to know that their reactions are logical, survival-oriented, or learnt from their family or social systems, we help them to make life make sense. When we can see our families' own history of conflicts and patterns of behavior, we can get a better idea as to how we got to this point in our lives. We cultivate self-compassion. It allows us to not be so hard on ourselves.

As one of the RAP strategies, we use genograms to visually clarify the legacies inherited from a client's family tree. It becomes easier to see what relationship patterns were adaptive or maladaptive. We help them to know the past is present. Knowing this helps us to continue what was most helpful and become cycle breakers for what was less so.

Racial Trauma Target History

Even after building a therapeutic alliance, learning mindfulness-based techniques, and getting to know more about our client, we're still at the beginning of our journey. Before we clear the traumatic events that are at the core of the trauma survivor's suffering, we need to strategically address the events that set the foundation of suffering in their lives. The impact of events during childhood have already been discussed in previous chapters, but other critical events happened even before the birth of the client. To address these, we must create the racial trauma target history.

There are events that are so deeply imprinted we don't always talk about them. The legacy of chattel slavery, family separations, imprisoned family members, losing loved ones to gun violence, being raised in poverty—there are a number of ways that indelible scars are etched into our spirit from the moment of birth. We need to consider this historical background in order to wrestle with the impact of racial trauma and the need for specialized therapeutic approaches like the Rhythm and Processing Strategies.

We make room not only for traumatic events at the interpersonal level but for difficulties that were out of the trauma survivor's control or that they were helpless to defend against. There are some that occurred at the outermost levels of the four cores of anti-racist psychotherapy. Through questions that touch on different aspects of a person's life, we can discover what pivotal moments hurt or defined them because of who they were.

The questions we ask can relate specifically to race, but most of them do not. Not every Black client has racial trauma. Race and culture can impact trauma, but they are not always the definitive source of the client's suffering. For this reason, we ask about traumatic events relating to childhood, adolescence, workplace discrimination, social identity, and even birth trauma.

There are many categories that we cover. But in the end, we create a list of experiences of shame, guilt, or other emotions that have caused our hearts to grow heavy. But even though there are many questions, our suffering is never endless. At the end of the process, we get a concrete number of trauma targets. This makes therapy manageable by keeping the end in sight. We revisit this list in future sessions to motivate the client to clear each target. By using the techniques in the next chapter, we can heal each of our trauma targets, one by one.

Summary

The adaptive information processing model sets the groundwork for healing traumatic events. We must recognize that all of us have the ability to adapt, improve, and recover. Traumatic events can become dysfunctionally stored in our memory, but it is possible to reengage our natural capacity to reprocess them.

Rhythm and Processing is more than a technique. It is the culmination of all the concepts described up to this point. There are strategies used to help orient a person to the present, improve motivation, assess for complex PTSD symptoms, understand the survival-based nature of the nervous system, and elicit the specific events that have led to maladaptive ways of coping with suffering. In the next chapter, we'll talk about the cycle that maintains the dysfunction, as well as the RAP techniques that help to bring healing.

CHAPTER 7

REWIRING RESPONSES WITH RHYTHM

Ancestral Resource

"I don't know what to do."

Camila, a therapist of Ecuadorean descent, exuded a soft strength as she sought my consultation. Her colleague was a white woman. They both co-supervised students at a local university. Although they both were politically left-leaning activists and my consultee labeled her as an ally, something was off. Students were secretly disclosing to Camila that their supervision was oppressive.

"Oppressive?" I asked. "Did they give an example?"

"It's like she's forcing the students to do therapy, but only the international students." Camila sighed.

"Did they try talking this through with her?"

"Are you kidding?" She nearly jumped out of her seat. "She would just deny it and insult you. Everyone's afraid of her!"

"Oh, man," I rubbed my chin. This was not unusual. Many people in workplaces who speak English with accents experience discrimination at higher rates than those who don't.[92] The students were in a vulnerable spot. It's a miracle they even chose to admit this was happening to Camila. Even though she was also a supervisor, they knew she cared.

"Well," I said, "have you thought about what you would say to her?"

"I don't even know how I would have that conversation with her."

---

[92] Hosoda, M. (2016). Perceived underemployment, perceived accent discrimination, and job attitudes among immigrants: The mediating role of perceived organizational support. *Journal of Organizational Psychology, 16*(2), 11–28.

A look of discouragement fell over Camila's face. She was facing a seemingly unsolvable problem. I didn't have enough information to give her the perfect answer, but I knew she did.

"Well," I said, "wanna try something new?"

"Sure!"

It was a clinical issue very different from what I had experienced in my own practice. Her workplace was different from my own. Our genders, even our cultural identities were different. What I would say would probably be received differently, and she believed that her identity worked against her. My advice wouldn't work on its own. We needed to develop a resource.

"What's an image that represents the essence of your resource?"

She thought for a moment.

"It's an image of my grandmothers, on both sides. They were strong women."

"What do you see in the image that represents strength?"

"They never gave up; they went through worse than me"—Camila became teary eyed—"and they still never gave up."

"Let's develop this resource and use the will of your ancestors."

She cultivated the image and then customized it. She took her time modifying every aspect of it down to the sound, look, and smell. Through a process of refining the image and changing how she felt in her body, she grew confident.

"How do you feel about talking to your colleague now?"

She adjusted herself in her chair.

"I realize I was tying my relationship to her with my job. They are separate. That conversation will happen on Monday, whether she likes it or not."

I nearly flew out of my seat with excitement. Her sudden change of perspective brought a smile to my face.

Camila's perspective changed so radically from just fifteen minutes ago. I didn't need to know the content of her thoughts; all I needed to do was facilitate the process. Now that she felt protected by her ancestral resources, nothing could stand in her way.

Camila's example gives us a glimpse into our discussion of how problems maintain themselves and how we can use our creative imagination to solve them.

In the previous chapters, we explored the foundations and rationale for anti-racist psychotherapy interventions. We need to understand the interconnected nature of people's narratives, the emotions tied to their everyday experiences, and the impact of their unique identity.

In this chapter, we will deepen our knowledge of how problems impact us and go over the resources that help us resolve the cycle that perpetuates suffering.

Intervention Strategies and Therapeutic Goals

The Rhythm and Processing approach alters negative beliefs by targeting core issues. But what exactly is the target? How do we do this efficiently? This is where the cycle comes in. The Cycle of Consolidation is an original concept that I first explored in *Racial Trauma Recovery*, which demonstrates how traumatic memories and external stressors interact and perpetuate suffering. The following is a model of how problems impact the trauma survivor.

Cycle of Consolidation

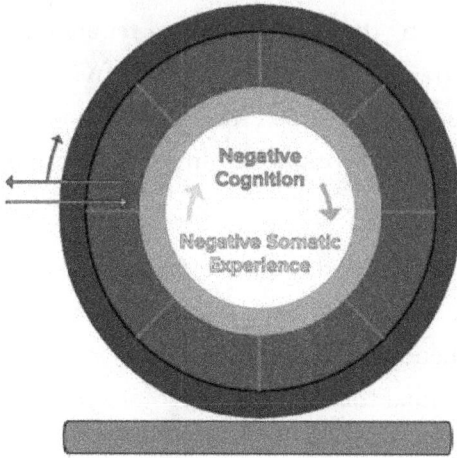

The image above shows a spinning circle hovering over a horizontal rectangle. The circle is a wheel, and its components are the hub in the center and the tire that surrounds it. The blue central layer represents the hub, the purple layer around it represents the spokes, which in turn connect to the outer black layer, which is the tire.

The horizontal line underneath the wheel is the road, which we'll get into later. What's most important is that the hub symbolizes people's distorted beliefs which are connected to feelings of discomfort about themselves.

Interaction of Mental Energy

Looking closely at the center of the hub are the words: "negative somatic experience" and "negative cognition." The energy exchange between them creates a feedback loop. Our negative thoughts impact how we feel, and how we feel impacts what we think about ourselves. They point towards each other in a circular motion. This causes the wheel to move, which initiates the "spin" or symptoms that people experience from trauma.

Interaction with External Stressors

The spokes (between the hub and the tire) represent the connection to the interplay with the near-limitless reminders and traumatic memories linked to negative self-reminders. When the wheel is in motion, the tire bumps against external realities, such as discrimination in housing and the workplace, microaggressions, and other environmental stressors.

The negative beliefs and negative feelings associated with them "connect" through the spokes with events that become stored in our mind as trauma. Whenever this happens—the contact of the tire and the road—there's a potential for trauma to become consolidated. This feeds into the cascade of traumatic reminders that reinforce maladaptive memory associations. The interaction between the wheel and the road represents the near-constant encounters with trauma triggers and external stressors. They reinforce the beliefs and also sensitize the trauma survivor to their harmful effects.

Centrifugal and Centripetal Concepts

The wheel analogy is significant, but there are also arrows on its left that represent the forces not always acknowledged in therapy. There is a centrifugal (outward) force that keeps the wheel moving and a centripetal (inward) force that pushes toward the center. The outward force is due to the person's internalization of oppression.

It represents the continuous interaction that a trauma survivor will have with trauma triggers and external stressors because of their identity. It works from the inside out and is based on the hub's interplay of negative beliefs and negative feelings, which keep the survivor constantly in contact with these elements. This arrow points outward and forces the wheel to turn.

But there is another arrow, one that works differently. It represents the inward force pointing toward the hub. This is a social force that promotes the internalization of oppression, drawing certain individuals to internalize specific negative beliefs about themselves that other people don't have or wouldn't naturally have as often. It works from the outside in. This is what makes survivors of identity-based stresses internalize beliefs that other people are less likely to have.

The interplay of these forces symbolizes the endless cycle of negative beliefs and feelings that keep the individual trapped in a whirlwind of trauma and stress. Now that we have identified the cycle of consolidation, we need to slow it to a halt. Let's dive deeper into the Rhythm and Processing approach so we can learn how to help people recover.

Rhythm and Processing: A Direct Approach

Rhythm and Processing Strategies are designed to cut to the chase and target what is stored in the hub. Without focus, therapy can take an endless number of sessions going around in circles, staying only at the fringes of the outermost parts of the wheel. Some approaches only focus on the therapist's interpretation of traumatic events, or even worse, cycle through endless validation scripts ("I hear you," "so what you're saying is," etc.). If therapists are not careful, they run the risk of driving blindly, with no clear path to recovery.

The problem that the client comes in with is not based on the content of their story but what keeps them in a problem state of mind. This is partly because their suffering keeps getting shoved into their faces, yes, but another important facet is that they believe they will never change. Alongside this entrenched belief, there is a heaviness in their heart, a difficulty with getting out of the bed in the morning, or a gut-wrenching sensation that emerges when they think of confronting their oppressor.

But what happens when we deal with these feelings? Without the bad feeling, the feedback loop stops. But not only that; it leaves room for encouraging feelings to manifest in their place. In the simplest terms, we need to heal the pain to make space for people to recover. We don't need to talk about the pain. We don't need to tell them their pain is in their imagination and they just need to conform. We need to give them the opportunity to notice their awesomeness.

What we change is how people feel about the problem, which in turn changes what they believe about it, and, when done effectively, clears the hub that generates the symptoms. We use this approach to avoid going in circles or trying to address the endless number of individual slights and stresses only to be expected in a society systemically discriminates. Let's not get distracted. Regain our focus. Deal with what initiates the feedback loop in the first place and stop the cycle.

Revisiting Memory Storage

Let's quickly review from chapter five. Information is stored in two main categories of memory: explicit and implicit. Explicit memory deals with stories, facts, and autobiographical information, while implicit memory stores emotional and procedural memories that are necessary for survival.

Keep in mind that these are not absolute categories, and there is much that is unknown about how memory works. But the general idea is that implicit memory is harder to bring up consciously than explicit memory. This is why it's very hard to do this if all we are relying on is speech from the client or verbal interpretations from the therapist. We need to turn it up a notch.

Proactive and Responsive Resources

Rhythm and Processing addresses the core that houses implicit memory information. We need to do this because trauma survivors usually have difficulty putting words to overwhelming memories. This is partially because of how traumatic memories get encoded and because of dissociative barriers that shut down the system as a result of feeling "overtaken" by fear, rage, or shame. So instead of focusing on specifics from the past, we must focus on what shows up in the therapy room.

Regardless of how a person remembers or anticipates a problem, they usually feel a way about it. If we feel emotional distress, we usually experience a physical sensation that accompanies it. Think about this. If something is a problem for you, your brain will give you a signal and this can show up in your body, your facial expression, or even in your mind.

This feeling, in whatever unique way it shows up, forms the rationale for using an alternative method to address the source of the trauma survivor's discomfort. Any way that your nervous system represents your problem is important, not only in terms of the body location, because it can even be felt outside of one's body, but also in terms of its intensity.

What impacts a person's stress level is whether it is within the threshold of what they can manage. We all have different capacities. Some may compare this to a window of affect tolerance.[93] This is a helpful concept because it helps us know that some people can manage certain stresses better than others. It takes a lot of energy to keep thoughts in awareness or to keep them from reaching our consciousness and not everyone has the same resources available to do so.

Complex trauma survivors deal with stresses differently than most people. This is because they usually have their resources depleted due to managing repeated stressors, being in near-perpetual states of hypervigilance, alternating between levels of dissociation, being constantly sleep deprived, or even being overwhelmed by the demands of daily life. This means that when they get stressed, it's much harder to

---

[93] van der Hart, O., Groenendijk, M., Gonzalez, A., Mosquera, D., & Solomon, R. (2014). Dissociation of the personality and EMDR therapy in complex trauma-related disorders: Applications in phases 2 and 3 treatment. *Journal of EMDR Practice & Research, 8*(1).

re-establish a baseline of calm than for non–trauma survivors. Stresses are harder to tolerate when we are lacking support. And this is why we need to find or create them.

Resources can be either proactive or responsive. Proactive resources are meant to address future stressors, things that haven't happened yet or are expected to happen. Responsive resources are meant to manage events from the past that have happened yet still cause a stress. Both allow a person to be more fully engaged in the present moment, which is exactly what trauma survivors need in order to feel more balanced.

The Strength of Creativity

Our imagination is powerful. The ability to imagine images, perceive solutions, or experience resourceful states of mind is incredibly useful. When we use resources, we can feel more integrated or whole, and this all comes from using our imagination. In chapter six, we discussed the polyvagal theory. On the same topic, Dana[94] suggests that it's possible for us to use visualizations to inhibit our autonomic nervous system's stress responses and create states of calmness.

Even without anyone nearby, remembering experiences of "reciprocity" allows people to experience connection. If our brain represents fear in different parts of our body, then naturally it does the same with the absence of fear. Our present thoughts are connected to our past experiences, and if our present focus is on warmth, safety, and calmness, then the body will experience it.

So look, I'm not saying we can just pretend to be a zen master with our imagination, but I *am* saying it doesn't have to be perfect. We just need enough so that we can feel something different than absolute fear.

---

[94] Dana, D. A., & Porges, S. W. (2018). *Polyvagal theory in therapy: Engaging the rhythm of regulation.* National Geographic Books.

If we can do this, then we can use our infinite creativity to overcome obstacles and change limiting beliefs.

Primary Proactive Resource: Resource Integration

Resource integration is a proactive resource technique. It is designed to prepare clients before they need to deal with the challenges of trauma processing. But it is also helpful for dealing with stresses in our daily lives. Here is a simple example.

Problem: Camila is concerned about a specific interaction with a white woman in a powerful position that may not go well or as expected. She feels discomfort in her stomach because of this. Her thoughts feed into her discomfort. She feels discouraged because of these sensations.

Intervention: By using resource integration, she cultivates an ancestral resource of her grandmothers. She feels inspired both literally and figuratively. She experiences a soothing sensation throughout her body. The feedback loop of the negative feeling and negative expectation has been challenged. We repeat this for a few rounds.

Outcome: She feels hopeful in her mind and lighter in her body. The content of her thoughts and expectations for the communication to change become aligned. She is back to feeling balanced and optimistic.

Using EMDR therapy, Shapiro [95] recommended a number of different resources. They ranged from listening to audio recordings to practicing visualizations of being imbued with healing light. The

---

[95] Shapiro, F. (2018). *Eye movement desensitization and reprocessing (EMDR) therapy (3rd ed.): Basic principles, protocols, and procedures.* Guilford Press.

preparation phase of EMDR therapy involves the use of bilateral stimulation in conjunction with these creative interventions. Resource development installation, developed by Korn and Leeds,[96] uses bilateral stimulation to "install" experiences of positive feelings, experiences of mastery, relational figures, or symbols that carry a deep meaning to the client.

Out of what Korn and Leeds created, and from my own knowledge of guided meditation, neurolinguistic programming, and hypnotic inductions, I created resource integration. This specific protocol is what we would call a "proactive resource," one that we can use before the challenge happens. It could be practiced between sessions, so we can be ready to use it whenever we need it.

While developing its use, I was looking for a way to integrate the five senses and deepen the positive sensations associated with them. This focused visualization would provide a counterweight to the negative somatic experience and negative beliefs arising from the cycle of consolidation. Instructions were then given to "integrate" with the resource itself.

The person visualizing would imagine merging with their best qualities, cherished ancestors, or forces of nature. I wanted the process to especially be guided by the Africentric dimensions with a consideration for nature, spirituality, and the unique rhythm of their personality.

While experiencing this resourceful state, clients are instructed to speak "words of wisdom." When people feel differently, they speak differently, so we take advantage of this and give them an opportunity to

---

[96] Korn, D. L., & Leeds, A. M. (2002). Preliminary evidence of efficacy for EMDR resource development and installation in the stabilization phase of treatment of complex posttraumatic stress disorder. *Journal of Clinical Psychology, 58(12)*, 1465–1487.

rewrite their own narrative. During the process, they use their infinite creativity to customize the visualization, down to the colors they see.

It is the client and the client alone who is the director of their internal movie. Therapists are advised to remain silent and only intervene when necessary. The slightest judgment or comment can impact the client's visualization. The role of the therapist is to make space for the client to recognize their potential.

Resource integration encourages an embodied feeling of deep relaxation, confidence, and support. This is what we need to disconfirm the limiting beliefs that reinforce hopelessness. Let's be clear: I want people to practice feeling awesome even if they think they don't need to. We need to take an active stance in disconfirming oppressive beliefs and discouraging feelings that have nothing to do with us.

Proactive resources can help us to deal with stresses before they come up or whenever we feel overwhelmed, but sometimes persistent thoughts are more deeply entrenched in our minds. They are often based on events from the past but can also be anxieties about the future. No matter their origin, in addition to proactive methods, we also need responsive ones.

Primary Responsive Resource: RAP Technique

The RAP technique is a responsive resource. It is designed to respond and deal with things that bother us in the present. At its core, it involves recalling, destabilizing, and re-encoding target memories. Using the process of memory reconsolidation, all of this takes place while the client is focused on something calming, neutralizing, or even inspiring.

Here is an example:

Problem: Camila is concerned because of past experiences of confronting white women in positions of authority. She feels a bad feeling in her heart whenever she thinks of confronting powerful people. She identifies a childhood memory of when her father beat her. The belief "I am not good enough" comes to her mind whenever she thinks about speaking up.

Intervention: Camila chooses a video of an elder doing beadwork. The RAP technique is activated. By using the memory reconsolidation process explored in previous chapters, she is presented with enough disconfirming exposures to destabilize the problematic memory.

Outcome: The memory fades, the feelings change, and Camila replaces her negative belief with "I carry my ancestors with me." She feels a resonant, warm somatic experience in her chest. When she tries to think of the memory again, she can only bring herself to the full feeling in her core.

The RAP technique is based on Thomas Zimmerman's adapted approach to Manfield's flash technique. Zimmerman noticed that some clients were unable to self-soothe effectively or reach levels of "zero" disturbance through other methods, including the standard flash technique.[97]

This led him to create the Four Blinks version of the flash technique. He did this to allow for an approach that was aligned with the principles of memory reconsolidation and to address specific challenges faced by complex trauma survivors and others who are impacted by structural dissociation. By removing what was unnecessary from other methods of

---

[97] Zimmerman, T. (2022, May 21). *What is different about the Four Blinks version of Flash.* Four Blinks version of Flash: An open approach to trauma reprocessing. https://fourblinks.com/2022/05/21/what-is-different-about-the-four-blinks-version-of-flash/

intervention, he has since developed one of the most streamlined ways of healing trauma for both individuals and groups. The RAP technique builds on Zimmerman's inspirational approach.

Because we are using our therapy with people who do not feel comfortable in their bodies, whenever possible, we need to promote integration. Not only do we give space to all of our senses (sight, smell, taste, hearing, and touch), we also need the other two senses.

The first of these is interoception, which Khalsa and colleagues[98] refer to as necessary for survival. This refers to our ability to notice our internal state. Dissociative responses discourage us from doing this, and for good reason: the body is often home to our negative feelings and beliefs. However, if we actually take the time to listen to our internal feelings, we can make better decisions in the long run. So our ability to feel our bodies is essential.

The second is called proprioception. Stepper and Strack wrote a landmark study about this.[99] This relates to how our posture, movement, and body's orientation in space can change how we feel. To simplify it, we feel better when we stand upright than when we slouch in a couch. We feel better when we smile than when we frown. Even if the results are not always drastic, to some degree we can change our feelings when we change what our body is doing.

Interoception and proprioception are important for EMDR therapy too. Clients are instructed to get a read on their somatic disturbances, measure the intensity of their suffering, and follow instructions from the

---

[98] Khalsa, S. S., Adolphs, R., Cameron, O. G., Critchley, H. D., Davenport, P. W., Feinstein, J. S., Feusner, J. D., Garfinkel, S. N., Lane, R. D., Mehling, W. E., Meuret, A. E., Nemeroff, C. B., Oppenheimer, S., Petzschner, F. H., Pollatos, O., Rhudy, J. L., Schramm, L. P., Simmons, W. K., Stein, M. B., Stephan, K. E., Van den Bergh, O., Van Diest, I., von Leupoldt, A., & Paulus, M. P. (2018). Interoception and mental health: A roadmap. *Biological Psychiatry: Cognitive Neuroscience and Neuroimaging, 3*(6), 501–513.

[99] Stepper, S., & Strack, F. (1993). Proprioceptive determinants of emotional and nonemotional feelings. *Journal of Personality and Social Psychology, 64*(2), 211–220.

therapist to make movements with their eyes or even with other parts of their body. One of the popular ways of using EMDR's bilateral stimulation is to get people to tap each of their shoulders in a manner known as the "butterfly hug." This term was first coined by Lucina Artigas during her work with survivors of Hurricane Pauline in Mexico in 1998.[100] Using rhythm, movement, dancing, or tapping isn't so unusual when the goal is to restore harmony in the body and mind.

The RAP technique takes all of what's been discussed into consideration. It is a healing method that I hope will one day change the world and how we understand trauma recovery. Not only is it a method that therapists can use to help clients, but I dream of the day it will be adapted to be used by paraprofessionals and community members to help with environmental disasters, critical incidents, and the everyday self-care scenarios of trauma survivors globally.

Summary

The cycle of consolidation demonstrates how stressful events get lodged into people's minds. Trauma is more than just a single event; it is an interaction between all of the cycle's components that reinforce the suffering. Negative beliefs create a feedback loop with devastating somatic experiences. This feedback loop is at the heart of psychological symptoms, thought intrusions, and other issues that accompany traumatization.

There are forces that increase the chances for certain people to become traumatized and an outward force that re-traumatizes them and keeps the cycle going. We break this cycle targeting implicitly stored information, using interventions that go beyond words and instead create experiences. Mixing RAP strategies with proactive and responsive

---

[100] Jarero, I., & Artigas, L. (October 2023). The EMDR therapy butterfly hug method for self-administered bilateral stimulation. Technical report. ResearchGate. https://tinyurl.com/2dv4yakr

resources, we can motivate trauma survivors to manage triggers, stay encouraged, and creatively self-soothe before, during, and after moments of crisis.

The RAP technique is a key component for complex trauma survivors, and we need to take our time and discuss it. In the next chapter, we will go into more depth on what it is, how it's used, and how we can use our infinite creativity to rescue ourselves from the turbulent waters of traumatization.

CHAPTER 8

THE RAP TECHNIQUE AND VISUALIZING VICTORY

Music to My Ears

A Jewish-American transwoman appeared on the screen, sharing the virtual therapy space with me. Her name was Alex. We were listing off the racial trauma target events, and although this kind of lessened the load, it wasn't easy.

Therapy was a sanctuary for her, but she carried trauma in her heart. Her struggles were deeply personal, intertwined with her religion, sexuality, and gender identity. These were parts of her life that sometimes led to conflict and most times led to societal misunderstanding.

"What's the name of the target?" I said.

"It's a phobia," she said. "Umm…"

She was hesitating. The atmosphere grew tense.

"You don't have to say exactly what it is. Name it however you'd like."

She let out a sigh of relief. Many of her trauma targets were related to shame. Maybe because of her identity, maybe because of her gender; maybe because of what she thought I thought about her life. Her eyes met mine.

"Can I just call it 'purple'?" she said.

"Definitely."

We don't need a play-by-play of the trauma. This protected her from re-living it. It was also a more humane, a more respectful way to reduce any possible judgment in the room while making a treatment plan.

We continued down the list. I asked her about different trauma themes, and we filled row after row of the spreadsheet. But something unexpected happened.

"Oh!" Tears started to flow from her eyes. We had anticipated this would happen. Listing the targets, even without explicit content, still led her to access a surge of nameless overwhelming urges stored in her implicit memory.

"You know what to do," I said. "Vacuum it up, contain it, and let me know when you're ready."

Within seconds, Alex used her imagination and moved the intrusive thoughts, bad feelings, and shame out of consciousness.

"Ready," she said.

We then used our technique. I shared a video on the screen and gave her instructions. In a matter of minutes, she was calm. Her intensity level dropped right back to a zero.

"I can't believe it," she said.

Tears fell down her face.

Sensing a shift in her emotional state, I leaned in toward the screen. "You all right? Do we need another round?"

"No." She wiped away her tears. "I never knew this process could be so painless. And I never knew it would involve listening to Earth, Wind & Fire!"

We both laughed.

There is a fear that people have about confronting their suffering. And rightfully so. Even if we're using the RAP technique, therapy is never easy. But this is why we needed something that Alex could make her own. This is why our therapy needed to be something we created together. Her tears let me know that even before working on the target, we were changing the course of her trauma history.

Therapy for the Next Generation

As we step into the new era of the digital age and ever-changing cultural developments, it is clear that our ways of relating to one another, especially our methods of therapy, must evolve.

Most youths are digital natives; many have never even seen a cassette tape or used telephones that can't fit in a pocket. Yet, most therapists still rely on methodologies developed decades or even more than a century ago. We need updated methods that not only reflect the latest scientific discoveries but also translate well to virtual interventions.

The shift to telehealth caused by the COVID pandemic caught many therapists off guard; however, we adapted. Switching to video calls helped many people access therapy who otherwise couldn't have. On the surface, virtual therapy enhances access, especially for people with visible and invisible disabilities. But there is an untapped potential in online interventions; this allows for us to incorporate music, images, and video to heal deep-rooted trauma.[*]

Our worldview also needs an upgrade. Projections indicate that by the year 2050, the population of Africa will have doubled from its 2020 figure, reaching 2.5 billion. Why is that important? Because it means that one out of every four people on the planet will be African. [101] Immigration will still be a thing. Climate refugees will still be a thing. Factors such as race, cultural origins, and social identity will only become more relevant. The problems people bring to therapy today are different from those of the past, and they might get even more intense in the next few years.

[*] Michelli Simpson is a pioneering Black American therapist of Brazilian descent. She was one of the early advocates for using EMDR therapy with telehealth. She has been doing this long before the pandemic started. Let's give recognition to the Black and Brown women in our field.
[101] Statista. (2023, April 28). Forecast of the total population of Africa from 2020 to 2050. https://www.statista.com/statistics/1224205/forecast-of-the-total-population-of-africa/

Considering all of these factors, we need culturally responsive interventions designed for the future. If these topics interest you, I hope this chapter inspires you as well.

Enter the RAP Technique

The RAP strategies were created to help therapists to better understand their clients, but also, and more importantly, to help clients to understand themselves. After years of working with racial trauma survivors and experimenting with interventions from mainstream talk therapies, I realized there was a gap. Even the standard variations of EMDR therapy, while bringing us closer to healing, didn't always get us across the finish line. This realization led me to develop a new therapy, one aimed at addressing both the root causes and the self-sustaining mechanisms of racial trauma in a humane, life-enhancing way.

I wanted a truly client-centered therapy. One that wasn't so focused on fancy clinical terms or trying to sound smarter than the trauma survivor. One that used our imagination and creativity to its fullest extent. One that could even make therapy feel *awesome.*

Neither the trauma nor its ongoing effects are the survivor's fault. They were traumatized without their consent. They didn't choose to internalize the beliefs that benefit their oppressors. The words "I'm not good enough" were never meant to serve them. The never-ending flashbacks overwhelm them with bad words, pictures, smells, or sounds, and the survivor has no choice but to desperately suppress all of this from consciousness.

Trauma survivors struggle with self-harm or with actions like over-eating, depriving themselves of food, or abusing drugs or alcohol just to change how they feel about themselves. Just to change the state that produces the negative cognition and the somatic experience that accompanies it. The mind is trying as best as it can to make sense of what happened, but it often lacks a key piece of the puzzle. The survivor's mind and body desperately want to heal but don't always have the right context to do so.

Taking this into account, we use our minds to instead visualize—and ultimately internalize—the positive resources that we deserve to experience. We use internal resources to feel how we would like to feel. We learn to feel good in the present moment, which disconfirms what we previously would expect from the future. We make it so we can smile for no reason, which differs from what we have been programmed to do. And we do it without forcefulness, without pretense—but with full authenticity.

Filling the Gap

While most conventional talk therapies are effective at exploring narratives, they are limited in their ability to process deep, existential threat-level trauma without the overwhelming, unexpected abreactions that accompany their discussion. EMDR therapy does this well, especially when performed by a trained individual who understands complex trauma. I have been trained in other approaches that can also do this—the emotional freedom technique, brainspotting, hypnosis, and many others that help people heal without diving into the narrative.

However, most western approaches fail to explicitly deal with oppression, culture, or the four-core context of the client's life. Also, when using other approaches, advanced training and workshops are necessary to fully understand how to heal complex racial trauma, and most of them completely ignore dissociation altogether. While more therapies now provide guidelines for working virtually and in-person, technology is sometimes an afterthought and the texts that popularized these approaches do not always mention it.

And while a multitude of frameworks explain the suffering of racially oppressed people, we need something that conceptualizes not only why we suffer but exactly what to do to prevent it and help people to recover. Rhythm and Processing both stands on the shoulders of its predecessors and addresses the gaps in conventional approaches to treatment. We need a new paradigm shift for the twenty-first century. The trauma survivor chooses how to heal and recover. The survivor brings us the answer to their suffering. They alone are their own savior; the therapist is only there to witness it.

What Is the RAP Technique?

Based on an adapted form of Zimmerman's Four Blinks version of flash, my clients and I needed something that could be used for people with PTSD, complex PTSD, and dissociative disorders. I wanted to create a method that would be helpful for people of African descent, Middle Eastern people, Asian and Pacific Islander people, European people, and Indigenous people from all over the world.

The approach had to be culture-independent so it would not run into the same cultural issues that led to the need to make adaptations to EMDR therapy[102]—in some cases, the therapist's prompts while helping clients process trauma using the standard protocol had to be changed depending on the cultural context, as English translations don't always line up with other languages.

Additionally, while different cultures may agree on what constitutes a capital-T trauma, this is not true for small-t traumas. Hence, we need to be sure that people could fully see their unique experience represented in the therapy. The following pages will explain how to use the RAP technique when working with people who have complex and racial trauma.

---

[102] Nickerson, M. (2017). *Cultural competence and healing culturally based trauma with EMDR therapy: Innovative strategies and protocols.* Springer Publishing Company.

What Do We Need Before We Get Started?

Assessment is essential. Before initiating any trauma targets, the following is recommended:

- Administering questionnaires, including screening for dissociative symptoms.
- Teaching proactive and responsive resources to manage present-day triggers or future adversities.
- Clarifying motivations for therapy and addressing obstacles to change or limiting beliefs.
- Creating a family history through use of a genogram to highlight legacies/patterns from previous generations.
- Generating a spreadsheet based on the racial trauma target history.
  - This results in a treatment plan that includes items that are priorities for the client and recommendations from the therapist.

After the motivation to go through the therapy is established and the alliance is forged for the betterment of the client, only then does trauma processing begin. By this time, the client should already have practiced using proactive resources like mindfulness-based methods and resource integration, as well as responsive resources such as the RAP technique. Outside of the RAP technique, clients might already have a wealth of helpful resources they can use, and they are encouraged to practice them alongside the therapist's suggestions. Still, the following sections will discuss the RAP technique and its unique contributions to the therapy.

Introduced as both a resource and the main intervention for RAP strategies, the RAP technique is designed to reduce present stress and, by using principles of memory reconsolidation, to use an individual's capacity for adaptive processing to re-encode traumatic memories in a way that restores peace and harmony to a client. To be more specific, it reduces both the vividness of traumatic memories and the emotional reactivity towards them.

When used as a resource, it decreases stress about events that are anticipated to be troublesome and also eases a person's general mood. When used for trauma processing, it can target negative beliefs and negative somatic experiences that fuel distress in the client's life. Following in EMDR therapy's footsteps, it can then be used to install positive beliefs of the client's choosing while getting rid of the negative beliefs that came packaged with their traumatic memory.

The client chooses a video, music, or visualization of their choice. The therapist then instructs the client to blink at timed intervals following a set sequence. In doing this, the client can rapidly transform their perspective of the past event. The length of time it takes to clear traumatic events is significantly reduced in comparison to other trauma-based approaches. And its use of bilateral stimulation allows the healing effect to generalize to other similar trauma targets that carry similar themes. There are fewer steps to follow and a more "user-friendly" operating method than in many other approaches, requiring less time to train people and increased chances of permanent trauma resolution.

The RAP Technique's Components

The RAP technique shines in its recognition of the client's unique personality, preferences, and their infinite creativity. In my sessions, I have seen dolphins, whales, and even penguins play role in trauma processing. We cannot predict what the client's imagination will call forth or how they will resolve their problems in the end. Similar to an improvised jazz session, there is a skillful rhythm that borders on randomness but still follows a structure to the trained ear. Because of this, it is not unusual for clients to surprise both themselves and their therapists, if they can show up authentically in therapy.

The RAP technique, though carefully structured, allows for infinite possibilities. Yet it only involves three main components: vacuum, container, and focus (COM video). All of these are based on a person's imagination, but the COM video can be either a literal video or an imagined experience that promotes an emotional reaction to destabilize the content of the traumatic memory.

The trauma survivor accesses a distressing memory and moves it out of consciousness. The therapist then guides them to focus on a calm or motivating video. They are then given instructions to blink their eyes, which creates multiple repeated exposures to disconfirming experiences. This sets the memory reconsolidation process in motion, which updates and transforms the memory at its source. You got the basics? All right then; let's go deeper.

The Vacuum

Let's do a quick review. As explained in chapter four, complex trauma survivors experience confusing and disorienting physical sensations. Plagued by dissociative responses which were originally designed to protect them, people who have experienced overwhelm commonly use substances, distractions, or other methods to change their feelings or completely numb themselves out.

Also with the cycle of consolidation discussed in chapter seven, negative somatic experiences are closely linked with the beliefs that engender and support them. These feelings are the closest we can get to the dysfunctionally stored implicit memory information that is at the root of the trauma, as explained by the adaptive information processing model of EMDR therapy. This is why we must consider somatic experiences to promote recovery.

The vacuum is a metaphor that is meant to temporarily move physical and emotional experiences out of conscious awareness. The therapist utilizes therapeutic ambiguity to allow the client to imagine something that would be suitable for them. Because it is so open-ended, some people will use actual vacuum cleaners, while some will whip out teleporters from alien civilizations or even bend time and space to accomplish the task. Creativity is welcomed!

A person's body and mind are never separate and extend beyond the confines of their physical structures. This is why it's not unusual for trauma survivors to report brain fog or dissociated body symptoms. In some cases, they might describe tightness in their bodies or even discomfort above or around their body.

The vacuum is designed to move all of that material out of consciousness, even if only for a moment. It can even be used for the "feeling" of intrusive thoughts, negative self-talk, or somatic experiences linked with traumatic material. This is why imagination is important. The client is encouraged to try something they have never done before. No matter what the content is, the vacuum places it into a container.

The Container

Trauma survivors struggle to find shelter from their persecutory thoughts. In the absence of calmness, they seek ways to hide their thoughts or compartmentalize just to get by from day to day. So when people hear the suggestion to "contain" or "put it in a box," they may misinterpret this as a form of avoidance. Compartmentalizing stresses is an unreliable way of coping and is different from what we are talking about here. The container we are concerned with gives us a place to put everything that was vacuumed out of consciousness. We contain our nervous system's reaction to the trauma so we can heal it without getting overwhelmed by it.

When trauma survivors even think about accessing their past, they also think they will be gripped by the fear, flashbacks, and everything else they're struggling with. This is completely logical; the memories were repressed for a reason. This is why we don't need to unnecessarily expose ourselves to harm. The target is accessed, immediately vacuumed up along with any physical discomfort, and sent away into the container.

The container is then sent as far away as possible and moved out of consciousness.

There is no one way to do this. Some will imagine teleporting a mason jar to the bottom of the ocean. Others will visualize steel treasure chests driven toward the center of the earth. Others have plopped their stresses into pyramids and sent them flying to the outskirts of the solar system. As you can imagine, the possibilities are endless. The key thing is that, however they do it, the stress is temporarily placed out of reach.

Because we can multitask and be aware of many things at different levels of consciousness, just "touching" the target and temporarily moving it out of focus still allows us to work with it. We do not need to provoke the activation of traumatic material, as is sometimes done in EMDR therapy, prolonged exposure, and other approaches to trauma treatment. We just need the stress to be in the container for us to work with it.

Just the vacuum and container on their own can give us a momentary break from repetitive thoughts, discouragement, and other pesky psychological phenomena. But the next step allows us to change how our body responds to all of this.

The Focus (COM Video)

While the stress is contained, the client experiences something totally different. They are instructed to seek out media of their choice, most often a video, to serve as the mode of healing. In *Racial Trauma Recovery*, I called this a COM (Calm or Motivating) video. Since writing that book, I have seen people use everything from viral videos to Japanese anime fighting scenes and even gospel music concerts. But it doesn't even have to be a video; it can be a piece of furniture, a cherished memory, or even a photo captured on the client's cellphone. Because it could be any of these things, including a video, it makes more sense to just call it "the focus."

The client's preference is paramount. Letting the client lead reduces the chance of resistance from the therapist trying to set the agenda on her own. Putting the client in the driver's seat helps them to bring their own individuality, their preferences, and culture into therapy. It's a two for one deal; we're bringing in disconfirming information through the structure of the therapy and the experience in the session.

While watching the video, the therapist will instruct the client to blink their eyes at specific times. This leads to multiple exposures, multiple disconfirmations, and a feeling of deep joy, relief, or relaxation. It is not uncommon for clients to take deep sighs or big yawns in my sessions. I don't take any offense to it! In fact, the yawns are usually contagious because both of our parasympathetic nervous systems are letting us know that we're releasing stress and tension. It's gentler with the client and gentler on the therapist.

The Result

After several rounds of scanning the traumatic material, vacuuming it up, containing it, and blinking while tuning into the focus, the client then re-consolidates the memory. The memory that was previously vivid, loud, and overbearing now becomes distant and subtle, and in some cases it disappears outright.

When people recover and try to access the original memory, it either no longer troubles them or the content of it drastically changes. It's different for everyone and sometimes it's quite beautiful. I've heard clients say they could now see themselves as adults walking their childhood selves out of the building where the trauma occurred.

Many times, it can be really surprising. There was this one time, after clearing a target during a practicum training, the participant said they saw "buddy Jesus" in a plaid shirt holding a thermos, just chilling in the place where the traumatic material was supposed to be. What was most hilarious was that the person telling me this was an atheist! We both found it hilarious. But hey, that's how their nervous system represented peace. Regardless of how it looks, once the memory is re-encoded in this new form, it can no longer bring up the bad thoughts or the bad feelings. And that's what counts.

Bilateral Tapping

There is much more to the RAP technique than I can describe in this chapter—I promised my brother Kevin that this wouldn't end up being another one of my super-long books— but there is one extra point to add. Because a criticism of the original Four Blinks was that the healing could not be as deep as in other forms of therapy, strategic parts of the process include bilateral shoulder tapping to deepen the emotional experience.

Bilateral stimulation is an essential component to EMDR therapy and also to its descendant, RAP. The "butterfly" tapping helps us to increase the chances of generalizing treatment results from one trauma target to other similarly themed memories. In this way, we get the benefit from deep level healing and EMDR therapy's depth of treatment results. The process of using the RAP technique, derived from EMDR therapy's eight-phase protocol, necessitates confronting negative cognitions, installing positive beliefs in their place, and verifying the completion of the target.

Rescuing Ourselves

Another distinct RAP component is its focus on "rescuing ourselves." When people can reliably reduce their distress to a zero out of ten, they are encouraged to offer encouragement to that "part" of themselves that remains stuck in the trauma. The client is instructed to offer "words or actions" to the past version of themselves. This promotes additional disconfirming experiences. In some cases, they could even teach the past versions of themselves resources that the adult self has, which completely changes the narrative of the past event.

Earlier this week, I encouraged a client to teach the past version of themselves the RAP technique, and we all watched a video of a tortoise eating a strawberry together. Now I can't be sure what it was, whether it was the reptile chomping down or her laughing to tears, but the target was processed using this method. As you can tell, smiling is a big part of this therapy. We are trying to completely change how we interact with trauma. We are trying to change what we expect so people can look forward to healing.

Summary

The RAP technique gives us a glimpse into a new trajectory for trauma recovery. It is a way of reimagining client-centered therapy while leveraging the inherent creativity and autonomy of trauma survivors. The core components of the RAP technique are the vacuum, the container, and the focus. Each of these come from the client and are instrumental in transforming complex trauma.

We can rescue ourselves from the repeated exposure to stories of deep suffering. The RAP technique puts the client in charge of healing, reducing the chance of re-living emotional overwhelm or the therapist's chance of being vicariously traumatized. We use the strength of metaphor, the infinite creativity of the client, and our limitless technology to invalidate traumatic memories and change our narratives.

Joy can have its place in recovery. Therapy can be a source of levity. We can disconfirm the structure of our psychotherapy as well as the content of our suffering. The next chapter will close this book with critiques, limitations, and other anti-racist reflections. It is my hope that these perspectives will help you to learn more, feel better, and inspire others to do the same.

CHAPTER 9

CONFRONTING CONSTRAINTS AND LEAVING THE COCOON

Confronting Unsolvable Problems

Tears welled up in her eyes.

Amira sat in the dim light of her small apartment. The gravity of the situation was etched into the atmosphere, and I could feel our sense of shared grief. Her homeland, now a site of conflict and fear, brought shakiness to her voice.

"It's no use," she whispered.

We were starting to work on an unsolvable problem. The risk of bombs being dropped on her homeland was increasing. She had to turn off her social media because the posts were too overwhelming. The radio and news weren't helping either. As far as they were concerned, her people were the enemy. We used a visualization, but the stress just wouldn't go down.

Amira shook her head. "It's not working."

She was frustrated now.

"What's going on in the body at this moment?" I asked.

She paused for a moment. "Guilt. I'm feeling guilt. How am I supposed to feel good when my little cousins are hiding from bombs?"

Her comment hit like a brick. What was the use of therapy if it just numbed out her suffering? There had to be another way. We restarted the process. This time, her resource would take the guilt into account while cultivating pride in her culture, her people, and herself.

"An image of me and my family is coming up." Amira's expression softened. "It was during the civil war. There is candlelight. Even with the lights being cut off, it doesn't matter; we are still together."

"That's awesome." I smiled with a touch of relief.

As she developed the resource by adding color, sound, feelings, and emotion, I asked, "And what words of wisdom come from your experience?"

She didn't skip a beat. The insight was already there, waiting for her to access it. "We'll always find a way to live our lives."

We tapped together from left to right, acknowledging the image that inspired strength, resilience, and pride in herself. It would be an anchor to the present that would reduce the impact of the social structure's gaze. A way to turn off the social media's noise. A visualization to help her to feel grounded during uncertainty.

There was no way in a million years that a therapist would have been able to guess that an image of an event in a war zone could help manage stress. But it was much more than that. For the therapist, it was a message of resilience, hope, and support. For Amira, it was the answer to an unsolvable problem.

"Thank you, David," she said, tears in her eyes, before leaving the session.

No need for arguing, pleading, or political analysis. The client is the owner of the solution to their problem.

The Journey Up to This Point

Anti-racist psychotherapy was a part of my life even before I was a therapist. Growing up as a young Black man in a racist society was always a political matter, so there was never a set time in my mind where this path started. But thinking back to the Black Lives Matter protests in June 2020, something awakened in me. Seeing the placards held up high, hearing the speakers chant slogans, and standing alongside the multi-racial crowd in the downtown plaza transformed me forever.

We were out on the streets during a global pandemic. At the time, it felt like we were risking our lives against an unknown virus while protesting against the status quo. People genuinely wanted to see a change. That led me to quit my job and start my private practice to develop this approach full time. I had no choice but to decide to solve this problem of anti-Black racism. So, I read, studied, and just kept writing and writing and writing.

I published *Anti-Racist Psychotherapy* in 2021, which was my response to a growing sense in my practice that racial trauma was not being adequately addressed by any of the therapeutic methods I had been trained in. That book gave birth to a philosophy of change—a new method of approaching the problem of anti-Black racism, a new understanding of how racial trauma manifested and how it could be permanently altered.

Black Meditation came next. It was born out of the necessity to help my people to heal. It was written in a context where structural issues regularly prevent Black people from accessing Black therapists, or at the very least, anti-racist therapists of any racial identity.

Racial Trauma Recovery became the training manual for how to use the RAP strategies. Inspired by anti-oppressive practices and the process of memory reconsolidation, it set the foundation for the integrative approaches covered throughout this book.

Black Mountain was the science fiction novel meant to consolidate my anti-racist ideas while bringing to life Japanese anime-like characters that I used to draw as a kid. Why? Well, why not? I am constantly thinking of ways to challenge myself, and I tried to write an awesome story that would not only bring joy but also share the ideas of anti-racist psychotherapy with my friends and family.

All of my books are designed to share knowledge and create disconfirming experiences. My original goal was to become the therapist I always wanted to meet. But through writing, that has also changed. My goal now is to one day train my own replacement. I dream of the day that my teachings can inspire someone to exceed what I've created and solve the problems of our imperfect society.

Cross-Pollination

The butterfly is a powerful metaphor. You can't look at a butterfly in the same way once you know that it came from a cocoon. Its metamorphosis only happens because of a complex process. Transforming from a tiny crawler to a marvel of the skies, all in one lifetime, can seem like a miracle of nature. Yet this is the regular life of your garden variety butterfly. Many of us are still crawling. But once we recognize our potential, when we witness transformations on a regular basis, we can't stop from knowing that we all have the ability to fly.

We need new perspectives in the twenty-first century. There is an emerging postcolonial, multipolar world. The racial demographics of North America are changing due to immigration and low birthrates. The continuing climate emergency that threatens the lives of millions will drive the movement of people across borders. Artificial intelligence might solve problems or create even more problems without appropriate checks and balances.

These concerns, and many others that never would have made it to our therapy textbooks in the past, are now showing up front and center. We'll need the right tools to help people with climate anxiety, refugee-related stress, xenophobia, religious and ethnic intolerance, casteism, and the complexities of racial trauma.

Global solutions will never happen within silos; this is why I am hoping that my work, which is a cross-pollination of my knowledge of software engineering, social work, family systems theory, sociology, and psychology, can inspire others to think differently about what the next generation can achieve.

The intersections are clear: mental health is related to racial justice, racial justice is connected to economic justice, economic justice is related to climate justice, and so on. Intersections are a part of life, so cross-pollination is necessary. This comes naturally for butterflies. So let's forge a flight path toward effective therapy and for the next generation to live effectively.

Healing the Child Within

The world must know that treatment-resistant disorders—complex trauma, complex racial trauma, and other underserved mental health concerns—can be healed if we ask different questions and use different approaches. These problems are not perpetual or unchanging, and there is always hope for improvement. Just the other day, a client came in to meet with me and I would like to share what happened here.

Sonia was a refugee, stricken with poverty and jobless because her education in her previous country isn't recognized by mine. Because of her traumatic circumstances, including vivid flashbacks caused by violence in her home country, she had become reliant on the social security net. Luckily, there was an arrangement made with a non-profit organization in the area; otherwise we never would have crossed paths.

Our first target concerned the first time she was violently assaulted. During the RAP technique's "rescuing ourselves" intervention, she described what she was seeing: an image of the adult version of herself holding hands with a child-like version of herself. They emerged from the darkness. She was bringing the child into the light, telling her that everything would be okay.

Sonia was nearly twice my age and suffered from incessant nightmares, fear, and grief both before her immigration and after it. But something changed after she witnessed this visualization. Tears formed in her eyes.

"David," she said, "I have tried for years and years to get that child out of that dark place. Every time I tried, bars would show up in front of me and stop me from going in. Now, all of a sudden, we use this music, and I could take her out of that place. I could see her smiling back at me."

This woman was transforming before my eyes. Her face, her eyes, something deep was changing in her. She unburdened herself of her suffering, and I witnessed it.

"David, God bless you," she said.

These stories must be told. I am a writer because the tearful gratitude that I receive week after week is something I want other people to experience. I want people to know they can rescue themselves from suffering. I want therapists to stop getting frustrated and getting burnt out. I want the world to know that we can all heal.

Clinical Limitations

Despite my successes, and the successes of other therapists who have consulted or trained with me, I recognize that anti-racist psychotherapy has limitations. Nothing is perfect. So this book would not be complete without sharing RAP's strengths as well as any potential limitations.

Motivation for Change

"So, tell me, what's your motivation for seeking services?"

"I don't know. My girlfriend said I should go to therapy."

"Yes, but what is your reason for setting this appointment?"

"I don't know. You tell me!"

The first practical limitation is that if someone doesn't want to change, they won't change. Although I love RAP, this is a limitation in all therapies. You can't force change. This is why, early in the sessions, it is important to determine the client's motivation. If someone is trying to prove that they can't get better, or that this method can't help them, then nothing will stop them from fulfilling their own prophecy.

Mental Health and Environmental Factors

> "I should be taking my meds, but I don't wanna. Don't you agree with me?"

Using RAP, I have seen impressive progress for clients with psychotic disorders. But this has to be said. Although I believe we can help everyone, most of my clients have complex trauma and mental health issues that don't require them to be hospitalized the whole time that we're working together. Although I have had challenging cases with structural dissociative symptoms, most of my clients are on the outpatient side of things and don't have the most severe, debilitating forms of dissociative identity disorder, for example. This doesn't mean that everyone can't improve; it just means that we need more research.

Even though I don't work in a hospital anymore, some of my best work has happened while working in collaboration with other mental health professionals, specifically family doctors and psychiatrists. Not every case strictly requires medication, but I have seen it really help in cases where people had especially challenging mental health issues.

But when people don't take their medication, it's not always out of neglect or a question of "client resistance." Some people's trauma responses, financial issues, or chaotic environments are so extreme they cannot focus on therapy or on practicing resources of *any* kind. In those cases, negative beliefs are easily reinforced, and destabilizing trauma becomes much harder. These are my toughest cases. So, while change is possible, it requires more creativity and takes more time for recovery.

Heart of the Therapist

"I'm not racist, but...."

Let's be clear, the race of the therapist (or of any of their "one" Black friends) does not automatically make their intervention anti-racist. If the therapist has not worked on their own internalization of racism, sexism, or any other oppressive idea, the client will feel it. Trauma survivors can pick up on insincerity because they have had tons of experience with betrayals. There's no easy way out of this. Therapists must work on themselves if they want progress.

A message for the secretly racist readers of this book: if you're racist, that's okay. Just say it with your whole chest. I get too many clients who have been harmed by therapists who didn't disclose their racism on their websites. If you want to work with diverse groups, then work on your nervous system's response to the roles of white fragility/guilt/savior complexes. Heal that first and then consider working with racial trauma survivors. You know, you can even find a RAP therapist who can help you process the trauma of whiteness. Thank me later.

I am very serious about this, though. No method can make up for the lack of a kind heart or a genuine desire to help those in need.

Theoretical Limitations

There are criticisms of anti-racist psychotherapy that are important to address. Of course, this isn't every criticism. People will always have criticisms for critical theories for all kinds of reasons. Anti-racism isn't the lightest topic to sit with at the dinner table, and I get that. But here are a few comments I have heard over the years.

Validation of Racism from Anti-Racism

> "Most Black people in the United States are not in poverty. We need to stop telling people that."

Agreed. We must recognize that not all Black people are in a never-ending cycle of suffering. Portrayals of anti-racist philosophy can inadvertently validate racism by creating and re-creating whiteness and a form of Blackness that is entrenched in suffering. Professor Karen Hunter and Dr. Greg Carr, who host the "In Class with Carr" YouTube segments, have taught me a lot about the importance of cultivating a positive Black identity.

In one especially memorable segment, they explained that anti-racism cannot build a pyramid. The pyramids in ancient Egypt took several years and required community engagement and participation. Keep in mind, they weren't built by slaves, as most people wrongly assume. The point is that we can't build something durable by perpetually fighting against something else. If all we're doing is identifying with opposition to something, as the word "anti" in "anti-racism" suggests, then we're stuck confronting oppression, identifying with trauma without building the structural capacity to overcome it.

Anti-racists must not only confront suffering but also prioritize healing from it. Just like the transformation that occurs in therapy, healing arises from the client's experience. When the racial trauma survivor visualizes their younger self and gives themselves a hug, this overturns the entire narrative of the past. The experience of reliving a moment and providing themselves with the compassion that no one gave them the first time around completely changes the narrative.

Each time a Black man heals from his trauma, he redefines his identity according to his script instead of following someone else's. If we don't heal ourselves first, we will follow the script of our oppressors later.

We must carry both a shield and sword to fight oppression and protect ourselves from it. In the name "anti-racist psychotherapy," we have both the will to confront suffering and the impetus to heal from it. Let's be mindful of this so we can build institutions that last without recycling patterns based on internalized oppression.

Barriers Created by Whiteness

"I'm not racist. You're the real racist!"

Wrong. These kinds of defensive responses are not just ways of deflecting from an individual responsibility but also proof of a broader misunderstanding of anti-racist discourse. Some white people feel very targeted by the language of anti-racism—just look at the backlash against all of the progressive gains of the past few years. It is much more than just white fragility.

There is a weaponization of "discomfort" that explains why many DEI specialists are getting run out of their jobs and perhaps why the Supreme Court decided to repeal affirmative action in higher education. Reactionary political pundits are trying to make this about an attack on white "people," and especially their children's futures. I told you back in chapter four, DARVO is no joke.

So, let me be clear: it is the *system* of racism that is the issue of concern. This is larger than any one person. Those who identify with "whiteness," instead of those who just happen to check that box in the census, often identify with a myth of whiteness created and sustained by powerful people with their own interests. When you actually take time to think about it, these interests actually clash with the vast majority of white people.

The myth of whiteness functions to preserve the wealth and power of the few at the expense of the many. More than a century ago, W.E.B.

Du Bois spoke about whiteness as a "psychological wage," in that it functions as a metaphorical payment that's dependent on the devaluation of Black people. This racial distraction keeps the majority of white people from recognizing their own exploitation by the capitalist system.[103] Keeping poor white people distracted, using them as a shield to fend off any resistance protects the smallest minority of rich people who don't care about the rest of us.

The impact of the myth of whiteness is vast, creating social problems for white people as well. The white body ideal leads to white women being the most harmed by anorexia nervosa.[104] Ableism harms white people in a unique way as well. White men commit suicide more than any other group worldwide, often because they lose privileges once they become "disabled" by old age.[105] White supremacy/insecurity is a glass cannon that harms others even as it destroys its user.

The origin of North American society is racist—it exists only due to the genocide of Indigenous people and the atrocities involved in the centuries-long European transatlantic criminal endeavor called the *Maafa*.[106] Our society is oppressive because of its structure, the silence of the institutions that betray us, and the never-ending racial disparities. So it's both logical and expected for people who identify with this society to imitate its beliefs, behavior, and trauma-laden history.

It's true, most white people aren't racist, but the privilege comes by not being targeted by anti-Black racism. This is why we say white people

---

[103] Du Bois, W. E. B. (2017). *Black Reconstruction in America: Toward a history of the part which black folk played in the attempt to reconstruct democracy in America, 1860–1880*. Routledge.

[104] Striegel-Moore, R. H., Dohm, F. A., Kraemer, H. C., Taylor, C. B., Daniels, S., Crawford, P. B., & Schreiber, G. B. (2003). Eating disorders in white and black women. *American Journal of Psychiatry*, 160(7), 1326–1331. https://doi.org/10.1176/appi.ajp.160.7.1326

[105] Canetto, S. S. (n.d.). Why white, older men are more likely to die of suicide. *SOURCE*. Colorado State University. https://source.colostate.edu/why-white-older-men-are-more-likely-to-die-of-suicide/

[106] Typically referred to as the transatlantic slave trade. This term was popularized by Dr. Marimba Ani.

benefit from racism. Still, at the same time, there is a growing progressive movement, especially among the youth, that is challenging the old guard. Most Americans are more progressive than politicians would have you think, and they are becoming increasingly so. The problem is that the old way of doing things is so loud, vocal, and prominent that the little minority of racists have us thinking we are outnumbered. Don't fall for the okie-doke. Don't let up. The momentum of change is on our side.

The Constraints of Racial Binaries

"I don't identify with any race."

This is understandable. The limitations of using traditional racial categorizations in anti-racist psychotherapy were brought front and center to me in an email from an Ethiopian reader. She wrote that she liked my books, but in her context, ethnic discrimination was more important than racism. Ouch. Well, at least she was nice in her email. But she has a point, and this is why we have to see race as being more than just about color.

In chapter four, we spoke about how the binary complex trauma cycle presents "white" and "black" in a metaphorical sense. For example, there is an Israeli supremacy affecting Palestinians, and a Hindu supremacy in India. Ethnic minorities in Australia, China, and Egypt also experience oppression. These metaphors are meant to address the universal yet socially constructed nature of the supremacy/insecurity complex. The flip side is that this can lead to real solidarity among all oppressed people, whose delegitimization and repeated victimization occur through similar processes.

Anti-racist theories on their own aren't enough to heal the world, but we need to start somewhere. Anti-racism helps us to understand the dynamics between identities, where some are placed on pedestals because of their language, race, gender, religion, sexual identification, ethnicity, and so on. But it needs to be intentionally intersectional so we don't pigeon hole our perspectives. We also need to be concrete about it so we can realistically improve the lives of those who are oppressed across the spectrum of identities.

So yes, this is all bigger than just the binaries of Black and white. If you don't like the words anti-racism, that's fine. Seriously. I'm not very judgmental about other people's opinions. Substitute the word for whatever you want. But let's not stop at semantics. Let's talk to those who are oppressed, and you will see that they, too, have trauma because of their identity. And it's worthwhile for them to know they can heal just like everyone else.

Limitations by Our Social Context

> "How am I supposed to go to therapy when I'm struggling to pay my rent?"

This is a tough one. Therapy is often seen as a privilege because those who offer it rarely live like those who need it. My career path required me to be in school for a large part of my life, and even though I was raised in a low-income household, there is privilege in being able to do that. Just like Amira and Sonia, the two discussed in the vignettes earlier in this chapter, I know that those who can't afford therapy are those who need it the most. Those of us who need social assistance programs, women's shelters, and child protective services are also those who deserve the highest quality of services.

Evidence-based solutions have shown some success. Integrated care models that make mental health care part of primary care interventions make healing more accessible. Mobile and virtual mental health services have been lifesaving for many, but we still need more. Ultimately, what we need is a new model, maybe one that brings healing into the community rather than outsourcing it to people who aren't from the communities that need the help. I have supported couples, families, and roommates to use certain techniques in a peer support capacity with great success. We need clients to become the best therapists they can be.

But the financial burden should not only be placed on the public. We need to reform policies. Many American therapists have told me that insurance companies practically run the mental health field. It's true that their influence is complex and varies by coverage, but the need for reform is clear. Policy changes like expanding government-funded mental health programs and reducing dependence on private insurance companies can make a real difference. Mental health must be seen as a human right; no one should have to choose between treating their depression and feeding their children. Think about it: why should people pay for health? Tax the rich. The same system that creates conditions for mental illness should cover the cost to heal from them.

As anti-racists, we need to push further to make these social issues a social responsibility. There is no reason why we can't envision better access to therapists, more Black mental health providers, more anti-racist therapists, and low-cost or no-cost, high-quality therapy. People are our most important resource. You cannot have physical health without mental health. We need to reshape our priorities by voting in politicians who can make change happen and voting out those who put profits before the people. Mental health is interconnected with the health of our society.

Reforms in mental health care are part of a larger societal need for change. Once our countries can stop dropping bombs, stockpiling weapons, ripping out the resources from the depths of the planet while forcing taxpayers to cover the costs of it all, then maybe we can redirect our focus to collective well-being. The challenges my clients face extend beyond personal trauma to societal and global concerns.

My clients literally think the world's coming to an end. What am I supposed to tell them using conventional approaches? Just go write about it in your journal? No. They deserve more than that. When women tell me they are upset because of gendered microaggressions at work, what am I to tell them? Don't be angry? Nah, forget that. I tell them it is human to be angry. Trauma survivors are told it is all in their head. So be it, then. Let us use our heads to change the world.

When we think about all these challenges, from climate anxiety to systemic oppression, it's clear that making opportunities for healing is bigger than health care; it's a necessity for deep, societal change. Let's start with making mental health a human right.

The Gift That Keeps on Giving

When people heal from their suffering, they become better advocates for others. Once we free ourselves from the psychological burden of dissociating from chronic and accumulated threats to our existence, we gain the energy to do new things. I want my clients to use their anger to move mountains. I want them to cry their tears to release suffering. I want them to leap to their feet and laugh out loud after we watch a video of dancing cartoon cats.

Let's experience the full range of the human experience, not just the societal labels or the betrayals that blight our existence. Heal from your suffering, re-learn yourself. Learn to love again, starting with the most vulnerable part of yourself. There is no greater gift than bringing compassion to ourselves.

Some relationships are dependent on you *not* loving yourself. Relationship partners tend to choose each other because of similar trauma histories or complementary ones. Addicts find co-dependent partners; abusers choose submissive people pleasers and all of them get locked into comfortable, familiar roles that are hard to break.

Whether we do this consciously or not, what happens if we transform our trauma? When we change, our relationships change too.

Either we change nothing and nothing changes, either we set boundaries and the relationship improves, or we stop playing the same games which can lead to the end of the relationship.

We exist in relationship to the four cores of anti-racist psychotherapy: individual/identity, racial trauma, family systems, and social/political. If we process our inadequacy at the deepest level, what happens? We may stand up for ourselves, ask for promotions at work, or even start our own businesses. When we re-consolidate the memories of the past, we're in a better position to change the future. When we lessen the load on our hearts, healing from the wounds we have sustained and self-inflicted, we break the cycle. As we cultivate compassion for ourselves, we have more to give to others. Compassion emerges as the gift that keeps on giving.

Be a Grandmother

It is true that anti-racism cannot build a pyramid. It is true that anti-racist psychotherapy cannot heal the world on its own. Not everyone is ready to confront their suffering. I get all of that. But despite the limitations, how do we stay motivated during these challenging times? This brings me to a client session I had a couple of days ago that really inspired me.

When faced with the stress of the climate emergency, Skye, one of my non-binary Mohawk clients, spoke about their helplessness. It was palpable, and it did seem hopeless at the time. There was non-stop news coverage of wildfires burning up so many trees that the New York city skyline was covered with shades of orange pollution—what was a therapist supposed to say? Just keep recycling plastics?

Instead, I urged them to use a resource specific to the concern in their body. The image that came up was of a 90-year-old Indigenous grandmother from their community. We built up the image, installed it, and integrated it. Then I asked, "What does the grandmother represent for you?"

In a split second, there was a shift in the energy of the room.

"She's a badass," they said.

"Oh!" I smiled. "Tell me, what makes you see her in this way?"

"Even though she is at the end of her life," Skye continued, "and even though a lot of the other kids don't speak her language as much, she and her friends make it a point to get together every weekend to create new words in their language."

I stopped.

I still think about this moment from time to time. Who was the therapist in that moment? Who brought knowledge to whom? I was reminded that anti-racist psychotherapy is as much about learning and listening to our clients as it is about maintaining determination. Just like the Indigenous grandmother who creates new words, we must continue to write, speak, and take action. Just like our ancient ancestral grandmother, mitochondrial Eve, we must brave uncertainty.

Although I'm speaking about anti-racist psychotherapy today, there's an evolution ahead of us. Life is ongoing, and even when it feels hopeless to fight against history, to take on oppression, or to deal with the state of the world, I hope you can stay determined. My clients are my greatest inspiration because they have shown me many experiences that can instill hope, create change, and find a way to solve unsolvable problems.

Summary

By revisiting memories from the past, we can reinforce them or heal them once and for all. *Anti-Racist Psychotherapy, Black Meditation, Racial Trauma Recovery,* and even *Black Mountain* call for a new paradigm that transcends conventional boundaries and addresses the root of complex and racial trauma. We need holistic, inter-disciplinary approaches that address the complexities of racial, gender, climate, and economic injustices. Every approach has its limitations, and no theory is above criticism. But let's not stoop down to cynicism because there are lives are at stake.

Think. Even in the face of adversity, how do we move forward? Why do we feel inspired after witnessing transformational change? What would happen we all experienced vicarious growth from seeing countless individuals recover from treatment-resistant issues?

There are problems much larger than racism that threaten our species' survival—war, pandemics, climate change, and other man-made disasters. We must acknowledge that what fuels these issues are not purely "logical" decisions but unresolved trauma histories that impact the thoughts, behaviors, and actions of those who create them. Even if it looks hopeless, nothing is really "treatment-resistant" when we use the right technology. Don't give up. Stay determined!

But in the same way that I started it, I also need to end this book with gratitude. Thank you. I never expected my words to reach so many people around the world. Remember, if the odds are against you, notice that discomfort. Tune into your infinite creativity and let's heal the families of this world. Even if we have inner child selves in need of healing, get in touch with that inner "badass grandmother" within. Take care, be strong, and fight for the future.

Blessings and Strength,

David Archer

INDEX

REFERENCE LIST

Acuña, R. (2000). *Occupied America: A history of Chicanos* (4th ed.). Pearson.

Adam, E. K., Heissel, J. A., Zeiders, K. H., Richeson, J. A., Ross, E. C., Ehrlich, K. B., Levy, D., Kemeny, M., Brodish, A. B., Malanchuk, O., & Peck, S. C. (2015). Developmental histories of perceived racial discrimination and diurnal cortisol profiles in adulthood: A 20-year prospective study. *Psychoneuroendocrinology, 62*, 279–291. https://doi.org/10.1016/j.psyneuen.2015.08.018

Alexander, M. (2020). *The new Jim Crow: Mass incarceration in the age of colorblindness*. The New Press.

American Counseling Association. (2023). Anti-racism. https://www.counseling.org/knowledge-center/mental-health-resources/anti-racism

American Psychiatric Association. (2013). *Diagnostic and statistical manual of mental disorders (DSM-5)*. American Psychiatric Pub.

American Psychiatric Association. (2021, January 18). APA apologizes for its support of racism in psychiatry [Press release]. https://www.psychiatry.org/News-room/News-Releases/apa-apologizes-for-its-support-of-racism-in-psychi

American Psychological Association. (2021, October 29). Apology for systemic racism [Press release]. https://www.apa.org/news/press/releases/2021/10/apology-systemic-racism

American Psychological Association. (2023, August 29). Racially motivated shootings in Florida add to trauma, grief experienced by Black Americans, says APA president [Press release]. https://www.apa.org/news/press/releases/2023/08/florida-racially-motivated-shootings

Anakwue, N. (2017). The African origins of Greek philosophy: Ancient Egypt in retrospect. *Phronimon, 18,* 167–180.

André, C. (2018). Phrenology and the Rwandan genocide. *Arquivos de neuro-psiquiatria, 76,* 277–282.

Archer, D. (2021). *Anti-racist psychotherapy: Confronting systemic racism and healing racial trauma.* Each One Teach One Publications.

Archer, D. (2021). *Black meditation: Ten practices for self-care, mindfulness, and self-determination.* Each One Teach One Publications.

Archer, D. (2022). *Racial trauma recovery: Healing our past using rhythm and processing.* Each One Teach One Publications.

Archer, D. (2023). *Black Mountain: Fight for the future.* Each One Teach One Publications.

Belgrave, F. Z., & Allison, K. W. (2018). *African American psychology: From Africa to America.* Sage Publications.

Bell, D. A., Jr. (1980). Brown v. Board of Education and the interest-convergence dilemma. *Harvard Law Review, 93*(3), 518–533.

Bierhaus, A., Wolf, J., Andrassy, M., Rohleder, N., Humpert, P. M., Petrov, D., Ferstl, R., von Eynatten, M., Wendt, T., Rudofsky, G., Joswig, M., Morcos, M., Schwaninger, M., McEwen, B., Kirschbaum, C., & Nawroth, P. P. (2003). A mechanism converting psychosocial stress into mononuclear cell activation. *Proceedings of the National Academy of Sciences of the United States of America, 100*(4), 1920–1925.

Bor, J., Venkataramani, A. S., Williams, D. R., & Tsai, A. C. (2018). Police killings and their spillover effects on the mental health of black Americans: A population-based, quasi-experimental study. *The Lancet, 392*(10144), 302-310. https://doi.org/10.1016/S0140-6736(18)31130-9

Borumandnia, N., Khadembashi, N., Tabatabaei, M., & Alavi Majd, H. (2020). The prevalence rate of sexual violence worldwide: A trend analysis. *BMC Public Health, 20,* Article 1-7. https://doi.org/10.1186/s12889-020-08580-3

Brenner, I. (2021). Disinformation, disease, and Donald Trump. *International Journal of Applied Psychoanalytic Studies, 18*(2), 232-241.

Canetto, S. S. (n.d.). Why white, older men are more likely to die of suicide. SOURCE. Colorado State University. https://source.colostate.edu/why-white-older-men-are-more-likely-to-die-of-suicide/

Carter, R. T. (2007). Racism and psychological and emotional injury: Recognizing and assessing race-based traumatic stress. *The Counseling Psychologist, 35*(1), 13–105.

Cavalcanti, T., & Tavares, J. (2016). The output cost of gender discrimination: A model-based macroeconomics estimate. *The Economic Journal, 126*(590), 109–134.

Cénat, J. M. (2023). Complex racial trauma: Evidence, theory, assessment, and treatment. *Perspectives on Psychological Science, 18*(3), 675–87.

Coates, T.-N. (2015). *Between the world and me.* Spiegel & Grau.

Cohen, L. (2020, September 10). It's been over 3 months since George Floyd was killed by police. Police are still killing Black people at disproportionate rates. https://www.cbsnews.com/news/george-floyd-killing-police-black-people-killed-164/

Cohn, D. (2015). *How U.S. immigration laws and rules have changed through history.* Pew Research Center. https://www.pewresearch.org/fact-tank/2015/09/30/how-u-s-immigration-laws-and-rules-have-changed-through-history/

Comas-Díaz, L., Hall, G. N., & Neville, H. A. (2019). Racial trauma: Theory, research, and healing: Introduction to the special issue. *American Psychologist, 74*(1), 1–5.

Dana, D. (2018). *The Polyvagal theory in therapy: Engaging the rhythm of regulation.* Norton.

DeAngelis, T. (2009). Unmasking "racial micro aggressions." *Monitor on Psychology, 40*(2), 42.

DeGruy-Leary, J. (2017). *Post-traumatic slave syndrome: America's legacy of enduring injury.* Joy DeGruy Publications Inc.

Du Bois, W. E. B. (2017). *Black reconstruction in America: Toward a history of the part which black folk played in the attempt to reconstruct democracy in America, 1860–1880.* Routledge.

Ecker, B. (2018). Clinical translation of memory reconsolidation research: Therapeutic methodology for transformational change by erasing implicit emotional learnings driving symptom production. *International Journal of Neuropsychotherapy, 6*(1), 1–92.

Ecker, B., & Vaz, A. (2022). Memory reconsolidation and the crisis of mechanism in psychotherapy. *New Ideas in Psychology, 66,* 100945.

Fanon, F. (1966). *The wretched of the Earth.* Grove Press.

Ford, J. D., Stockton, P., Kaltman, S., & Green, B. L. (2006). Disorders of extreme stress (DESNOS) symptoms are associated with type and severity of interpersonal trauma exposure in a sample of healthy young women. *Journal of Interpersonal Violence, 21*(11), 1399–1416.

Fredrickson, G. M. (with Camarillo, A.) (2015). *Racism: A short history.* Princeton University Press. (Original work published 2002)

García-Moreno, C., Pallitto, C., Devries, K., Stöckl, H., Watts, C., & Abrahams, N. (2013). Global and regional estimates of violence against women: Prevalence and health effects of intimate partner violence and non-partner sexual violence. World Health Organization.

Gómez, J. M. (2017). Cultural betrayal trauma theory [unpublished doctoral dissertation]. University of Oregon.

Gómez, J. M. (2023). *The cultural betrayal of Black women and girls: A Black feminist approach to healing from sexual abuse* (pp. xvii–236). American Psychological Association.

Gorski, P. C., & Erakat, N. (2019). Racism, whiteness, and burnout in antiracism movements: How white racial justice activists elevate burnout in racial justice activists of color in the United States. *Ethnicities, 19*(5), 784–808.

Grasser, L. R., & Jovanovic, T. (2022). Neural impacts of stigma, racism, and discrimination. *Biological Psychiatry: Cognitive Neuroscience and Neuroimaging, 7*(12), 1225–1234.

Green, M. J., Sonn, C. C., & Matsebula, J. (2007). Reviewing whiteness: Theory, research, and possibilities. *South African Journal of Psychology, 37*(3), 389–419.

Hall, H. (2022). Dissociation and misdiagnosis of schizophrenia in populations experiencing chronic discrimination and social defeat. *Journal of Trauma & Dissociation*, 1–15.

Harnett, N. G. (2020). Neurobiological consequences of racial disparities and environmental risks: A critical gap in understanding psychiatric disorders. *Neuropsychopharmacology, 45*(8), 1247–1250.

Harsey, S., & Freyd, J. J. (2020). Deny, attack, and reverse victim and offender (DARVO): what is the influence on perceived perpetrator and victim credibility? *Journal of Aggression, Maltreatment & Trauma, 29*(8), 897–916.

Herman, J. L. (1992). Complex PTSD: A syndrome in survivors of prolonged and repeated trauma. *Journal of Traumatic Stress, 5*(3), 377-391.

Hosoda, M. (2016). Perceived underemployment, perceived accent discrimination, and job attitudes among immigrants: The mediating role of perceived organizational support. *Journal of Organizational Psychology, 16*(2), 11–28.

Howell, E. A. (2018). Reducing disparities in severe maternal morbidity and mortality. *Clinical Obstetrics and Gynecology, 61*(2), 387–399.

Jarero, I., & Artigas, L. (October 2023). The EMDR therapy butterfly hug method for self-administered bilateral stimulation. Technical report. ResearchGate. https://tinyurl.com/2dv4yakr

Keating, L., Muller, R. T., & Wyers, C. (2021). LGBTQ+ people's experiences of barriers and welcoming factors when accessing and attending intervention for psychological trauma. *Journal of LGBTQ Issues in Counseling, 15*(1), 77–92.

Khalsa, S. S., Adolphs, R., Cameron, O. G., Critchley, H. D., Davenport, P. W., Feinstein, J. S., Feusner, J. D., Garfinkel, S. N., Lane, R. D., Mehling, W. E., Meuret, A. E., Nemeroff, C. B., Oppenheimer, S., Petzschner, F. H., Pollatos, O., Rhudy, J. L., Schramm, L. P., Simmons, W. K., Stein, M. B., Stephan, K. E., Van den Bergh, O., Van Diest, I., von Leupoldt, A., & Paulus, M. P. (2018). Interoception and mental health: a roadmap. *Biological Psychiatry: Cognitive Neuroscience and Neuroimaging, 3*(6), 501–513.

Kim, J. Y., & Meister, A. (2023). Microaggressions, interrupted: The experience and effects of gender microaggressions for women in STEM. *Journal of Business Ethics, 185*(3), 513–531.

King, T. (2017). *The inconvenient Indian illustrated: A curious account of native people in North America.* Doubleday Canada.

Knefel, M., Lueger-Schuster, B., Karatzias, T., Shevlin, M., & Hyland, P. (2019). From child maltreatment to ICD-11 complex post-traumatic stress symptoms: The role of emotion regulation and re-victimisation. *Journal of Clinical Psychology, 75*(3), 392–403.

Korn, D. L., & Leeds, A. M. (2002). Preliminary evidence of efficacy for EMDR resource development and installation in the stabilization phase of treatment of complex posttraumatic stress disorder. *Journal of Clinical Psychology, 58*(12), 1465–1487.

La Raza Database Research Project. (2023). 2023 Final Report. https://www.csusb.edu/sites/default/files/RazaDatabase%20Report%20Final%20Version%20-min.pdf

Leeds, A. M. (2016). *A guide to the standard EMDR therapy protocols for clinicians, supervisors, and consultants* (2nd ed.). Springer Publishing Company.

Levine, P. A. (2015). *Trauma and memory: Brain and body in a search for the living past: A practical guide for understanding and working with traumatic memory.* North Atlantic Books.

Linnaeus, C. (1964). *Systema Naturae* (10th ed., Vol. 45). J. Cramer; Stechert-Hafner Service Agency. (Original work published 1759)

Marich, J. (2023). *Dissociation made simple: A stigma-free guide to embracing your dissociative mind and navigating daily life.* North Atlantic Books.

Massey, D. S. (2017a). Segregation and stratification: A biosocial perspective. In K. M. Beaver & A. Walsh (Eds.), *Biosocial Theories of Crime* (pp. 49–67). Routledge.

McClendon, J., Kressin, N., Perkins, D., Copeland, L. A., Finley, E. P., & Vogt, D. (2021). The impact of discriminatory stress on changes in posttraumatic stress severity at the intersection of race/ethnicity and gender. *Journal of Trauma & Dissociation, 22*(2), 170–187.

McEwen, B. S. (2006). Protective and damaging effects of stress mediators: central role of the brain. *Dialogues in Clinical Neuroscience, 8*(4), 367–381.

Menakem, R. (2021). *My grandmother's hands: Racialized trauma and the pathway to mending our hearts and bodies.* Penguin.

Michopoulos, V., Powers, A., Gillespie, C. F., Ressler, K. J., & Jovanovic, T. (2017). Inflammation in fear- and anxiety-based disorders: PTSD, GAD, and beyond. *Neuropsychopharmacology, 42*(1), 254–270.

Miller, W. R., & Rollnick, S. (2002). *Motivational interviewing: Preparing people for change.* Guilford Press.

Miller, R. J. (2019). The doctrine of discovery: The international law of colonialism. *Indigenous Peoples' JL Culture & Resistance, 5*(1), 35–42.

Mukhopadhyay, C. C. (2008). Getting rid of the word "Caucasian." In M. Pollack (Ed.), *Everyday antiracism: Getting real about race in school* (pp. 12–16). The New Press.

Nguyen, T. T., Criss, S., Michaels, E. K., Cross, R. I., Michaels, J. S., Dwivedi, P., Huang, D., Hsu, E., Mukhija, K., Nguyen, L. H., Yardi, I., Allen, A. M., Nguyen, Q. C. & Gee, G. C. (2021). Progress and push-back: How the killings of Ahmaud Arbery, Breonna Taylor, and George Floyd impacted public discourse on race and racism on Twitter. *SSM - Population Health, 15*, 100922.

Nickerson, M. (2017). *Cultural competence and healing culturally based trauma with EMDR therapy: Innovative strategies and protocols.* Springer Publishing Company.

Oikkonen, V. (2015). Mitochondrial Eve and the affective politics of human ancestry: Winner of the 2015 Catharine Stimpson prize for outstanding feminist scholarship. *Signs: Journal of Women in Culture and Society, 40*(3), 747–772.

Owen, J., Tao, K. W., Imel, Z. E., Wampold, B. E., & Rodolfa, E. (2014). Addressing racial and ethnic microaggressions in therapy. *Professional Psychology: Research and Practice, 45*(4), 283–290.

Peatling, G. K. (2005). The Whiteness of Ireland under and after the Union. *Journal of British Studies, 44*(1), 115–133.

Perroud, N., Rutembesa, E., Paoloni-Giacobino, A., Mutabaruka, J., Mutesa, L., Stenz, L., Malafosse, A., & Karege, F. (2014). The Tutsi genocide and transgenerational transmission of maternal stress: Epigenetics and biology of the HPA axis. *The World Journal of Biological Psychiatry, 15*(4), 334–345.

Rose, S. (2009). Darwin, race, and gender. *EMBO reports, 10*(4), 297-298.

Said, E. W. (1979). *Orientalism.* Vintage.

Salter, M., & Hall, H. (2021). Reducing shame, promoting dignity: A model for the primary prevention of complex post-traumatic stress disorder. *Trauma, Violence, & Abuse, 23*(3), 906–919.

Schwartz, R. C., & Sweezy, M. (2019). *Internal family systems therapy.* Guilford Publications.

Shapiro, F. (2018). *Eye movement desensitization and reprocessing (EMDR) therapy (3rd ed.): Basic principles, protocols, and procedures.* Guilford Press.

Shengold, L. (1991). *Soul murder: The effects of childhood abuse and deprivation.* BoD–Books on Demand.

Shonkoff, J. P., Boyce, W. T., & McEwen, B. S. (2009). Neuroscience, molecular biology, and the childhood roots of health disparities: Building a new framework for health promotion and disease prevention. JAMA, 301(21), 2252–2259.

Siegel, D. J. (2012). *The developing mind: How relationships and the brain interact to shape who we are* (2nd ed.). Guilford Press.

Smith, C. P., & Freyd, J. J. (2013). Dangerous safe havens: Institutional betrayal exacerbates sexual trauma. *Journal of Traumatic Stress,* 26(1), 119–124.

Spiro, J. (2009). *Defending the master race: Conservation, eugenics, and the legacy of Madison Grant.* University of Vermont Press.

Statista. (2023, April 28). *Forecast of the total population of Africa from 2020 to 2050.* https://www.statista.com/statistics/1224205/forecast-of-the-total-population-of-africa/

Stepper, S., & Strack, F. (1993). Proprioceptive determinants of emotional and nonemotional feelings. *Journal of Personality and Social Psychology*, 64(2), 211–220.

Striegel-Moore, R. H., Dohm, F. A., Kraemer, H. C., Taylor, C. B., Daniels, S., Crawford, P. B., & Schreiber, G. B. (2003). Eating disorders in white and black women. *American Journal of Psychiatry*, 160(7), 1326–1331. https://doi.org/10.1176/appi.ajp.160.7.1326

Takei, G., Eisinger, J., & Scott, S. (2019). *They called us enemy.* Top Shelf Productions.

United Nations High Commissioner for Refugees. (2012). *Working with men and boy survivors of sexual and gender-based violence in forced displacement.*

van der Kolk, B. (2015). *The body keeps the score: Mind, brain and body in the transformation of trauma.* New York, NY: Penguin Random House.

van der Hart, O., Groenendijk, M., Gonzalez, A., Mosquera, D., & Solomon, R. (2014). Dissociation of the personality and EMDR therapy in complex trauma-related disorders: Applications in phases 2 and 3 treatment. *Journal of EMDR Practice & Research*, 8(1).

van der Hart, O., Nijenhuis, E. R., & Steele, K. (2006). *The haunted self: Structural dissociation and the treatment of chronic traumatization.* Norton.

Weikart, R. (2004). *From Darwin to Hitler: Evolutionary ethics, eugenics, and racism in Germany.* Palgrave Macmillan.

Welsing, F. C. (1991). *The Isis (Yssis) papers.* Third World Press.

Whitman, J. Q. (2017). *Hitler's American model: The United States and the making of Nazi race law.* Princeton University Press.

Williams, E. (2021). *Capitalism and Slavery.* UNC Press Books.

Williams, M. T. (2020). *Managing microaggressions: Addressing everyday racism in therapeutic spaces.* Oxford Academic.

Williams, M. T., Faber, S. C., & Duniya, C. (2022). Being an anti-racist clinician. *The Cognitive Behaviour Therapist*, 15, Article e19.

Williams, M. T., Holmes, S., Zare, M., Haeny, A., & Faber, S. (2022). An evidence-based approach for treating stress and trauma due to racism. *Cognitive and Behavioral Practice*, 30(4), 565–588.

Williams, M. T., Kanter, J. W., Peña, A., Ching, T. H., & Oshin, L. (2020). Reducing microaggressions and promoting interracial connection: The racial harmony workshop. *Journal of Contextual Behavioral Science*, 16, 153–161.

Williams, M. T., Skinta, M. D., & Martin-Willett, R. (2021). After Pierce and Sue: A revised racial microaggressions taxonomy. *Perspectives on Psychological Science, 16*(5), 991–1007.

Yehuda, R., Daskalakis, N. P., Bierer, L. M., Bader, H. N., Klengel, T., Holsboer, F., & Binder, E. B. (2016). Holocaust exposure induced intergenerational effects on FKBP5 methylation. *Biological Psychiatry, 80*(5), 372–380.

Zia-Ebrahimi, R. (2011). Self-orientalization and dislocation: The uses and abuses of the "Aryan" discourse in Iran. *Iranian Studies, 44*(4), 445–472.

Zimmerman, T. (2022, May 21). What is different about the Four Blinks version of Flash. *Four Blinks version of Flash: An open approach to trauma reprocessing*. https://fourblinks.com/2022/05/21/what-is-different-about-the-four-blinks-version-of-flash/

OTHER BOOKS BY THIS AUTHOR

If you liked **Transforming Complex Trauma,** you might also like its inspirations.

Anti-Racist Psychotherapy: Confronting Systemic Racism and Healing Racial Trauma
https://amzn.to/3b0iqvT

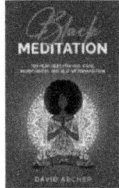

Black Meditation: Ten Practices for Self-Care, Mindfulness, and Self-Determination
https://amzn.to/3JEnhm7

Racial Trauma Recovery: Healing Our Past Using Rhythm and Processing
https://amzn.to/3C8HY89

Black Mountain: Fight for the Future
http://amzn.to/3qhKTYP

LET'S WORK TOGETHER

David Archer is available for podcasts, presentations, and trainings.

Let's deliver the message of **Transforming Complex Trauma** to those who need it.

Email me at david@archertherapy.com for more information. EMDR therapy certification, workshops, and free resources (mailing list, videos, and recorded podcasts) are available at:

www.transformingcomplextrauma.com

ARCHER
THERAPY

To connect with David Archer, access more content, or inquire about professional consultations or workshop presentations, please visit:

Website: https://archertherapy.com

Facebook: https://facebook.com/archertherapy

Instagram: https://www.instagram.com/archertherapy/

YouTube: https://www.youtube.com/@archertherapy

LinkedIn: https://www.linkedin.com/in/archertherapy/

If you like any of his work, please like, subscribe, write reviews and get the word out. Let's make a difference for the next generation of revolutionary therapists and awesome therapy-seekers. Thank you.

Be well, stay healthy, and take care.

www.ingramcontent.com/pod-product-compliance
Lightning Source LLC
Chambersburg PA
CBHW062133040426

42335CB00039B/2099